FIVE WALKS THROUGH MONTPELIER

WHAT ARE YOU LOOKING AT?!

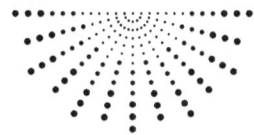

KATHRYN GUARE

KILTUMPER
CLOSE
PRESS

Copyright © 2019 by Kathryn Guare

All rights reserved.

ISBN 978-0-9911893-8-0

No part of this book may be reproduced in any form or by any electronic or mechanical means, including information storage and retrieval systems, without written permission from the author, except for the use of brief quotations in a book review.

The information in this book is true and complete to the best of our knowledge. It is offered without guarantee on the part of the author or Kiltumper Close Press. The author and Kiltumper Close Press disclaim liability in connection with the use of this book.

Kiltumper Close Press, Montpelier, VT

ALSO BY KATHRYN GUARE

Susepense Novels
The Conor McBride Series:
Deceptive Cadence (Book 1)
The Secret Chord (Book 2)
City of a Thousand Spies (Book 3)

Historical Novel
Where A Wave Meets the Shore

Audio Tours (narrated by the author)
An audiobook of all 5 tours is available at:

CONTENTS

Meet Your Guide	1
Tour 1 - The Capitol Complex	3
Stop 1.1 - A Quick Historical Overview	4
Stop 1.2 - A Painted Lady	8
Stop 1.3 - A Most Beautiful Tax Department	10
Stop 1.4 - A Country Doctor and a Hometown Hero	13
Stop 1.5 - Floods, Fires and Goddesses	19
Stop 1.6 - On the Edge of Where Private Life Begins	24
Stop 1.7 - The Keeley Cure	26
Stop 1.8 - The Grand Old Lady	28
Tour 2 - The Shopping District	33
Stop 2.1 - The Capitol Plaza's Ancestors	34
Stop 2.2 - A Murder and a Ghost Story	38
Stop 2.3 - A Green Space for Everyone	42
Stop 2.4 - An Invisible Bridge	43
Stop 2.5 - State Street Eateries	45
Stop 2.6 - Let's Talk About Blocks	48
Stop 2.7 - Crossroads of the Capital	51
Stop 2.8 - The Secret in the Middle	56
Tour 3 - Elm Street Mini Loop	59
Stop 3.1 - Mail Order Lockups	60
Stop 3.2 - Founders and Oddfellows	62
Stop 3.3 - The Old (Love) Triangle	64
Stop 3.4 - An Uncommon View	68
Stop 3.5 - The Intersection of Faith	71
Stop 3.6 - The Kellogg-Hubbard Hubbub	74
Stop 3.7 - A Baker's Dozen…Of Lawyers?!	78
Stop 3.8 - From Near Beer to Craft Beer	80
Stop 3.9 - It Ain't the Ritz	83
Tour 4 - Elm Street Extended Loop	87
Stop 4.1 - Elm Street Cemetery	88
Stop 4.2 - Our Big, Fat, Greek Love Affair	91

Stop 4.3 - A Butcher, Then a Baker	92
Stop 4.4 - Attractions Farther Afield	94
Stop 4.5 - What IS a Sawmill, Anyway?!	97
Stop 4.6 - The Birth of 2x4 Lumber	98
Stop 4.7 - Around We Go	102
Stop 4.8 - A Creditor, A Senator and a Carpenter Walk into a Hotel…	104
Stop 4.9 - Montpelier's "Arms Dealer"	107
Tour 5 - Stonecutters Way	111
Stop 5.1 - A Dive for Nice People	112
Stop 5.2 - The Firehouse That Came After the Fire	114
Stop 5.3 - Montpelier's Own Big Dig	116
Stop 5.4 - Baldwin's Last Laugh & Some Railroad Talk	120
Stop 5.5 - The Cross That Didn't Belong	123
Stop 5.6 - The Self-Taught Master	126
Stop 5.7 - Montpelier's Deep-Rooted Immigrant Community	130
Stop 5.8 - Remembering Our City in the Railroad Times	133
Tour 5 Map (continued)	137
Stop 5.9 - Got Any Heady?	138
Stop 5.10 - Somebody Had to Make Them	140
Stop 5.11 - You Won't Believe Whats On Tap!	142
Don't Go Yet	144

MEET YOUR GUIDE

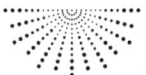

*H*i there!
My name is Kathryn Guare, and I'm going to be your local guide on these walks through Montpelier.

This is my hometown, so whether it's your first time here, or you're a regular visitor, or even a resident, I'm delighted that you're interested in learning more about the city, so thank you for letting me tag along to share some thoughts while you explore.

Before we get started I'll explain how these tours will work.

There are 5 walking tours in this series on Montpelier, and each numbered stop identifies the location where we're standing when the narrative begins. I've added a map at the beginning of each tour as a visual reference for each stop.

The tours don't have to be followed in order, but the narrative will make the most sense if you take the *individual stops* in order. However, if you are already standing somewhere else and - as the title suggests -

you just want to know what you're looking at, you can choose skip to the stop associated with that location and get the general gist of things. To make it easier to know where you are, the stops are numbered with both the tour number and stop number. So the first stop on this tour will be 1.1. The first on Tour 2 will be 2.1, and so on.

What will I talk about? Well, I'm going to try not to get too far into the weeds on anything. I'll be dishing out a little history and some information about what's happening in Montpelier right now. There will be a few stories, and shout-outs for stores and restaurants you may want to check out while you're here in the city, both well-known and off the beaten path. And I'll tell you where the public restrooms are. Are you ready? Let's get started!

TOUR 1 - THE CAPITOL COMPLEX

PAINTED LADIES AND HOMETOWN HEROES

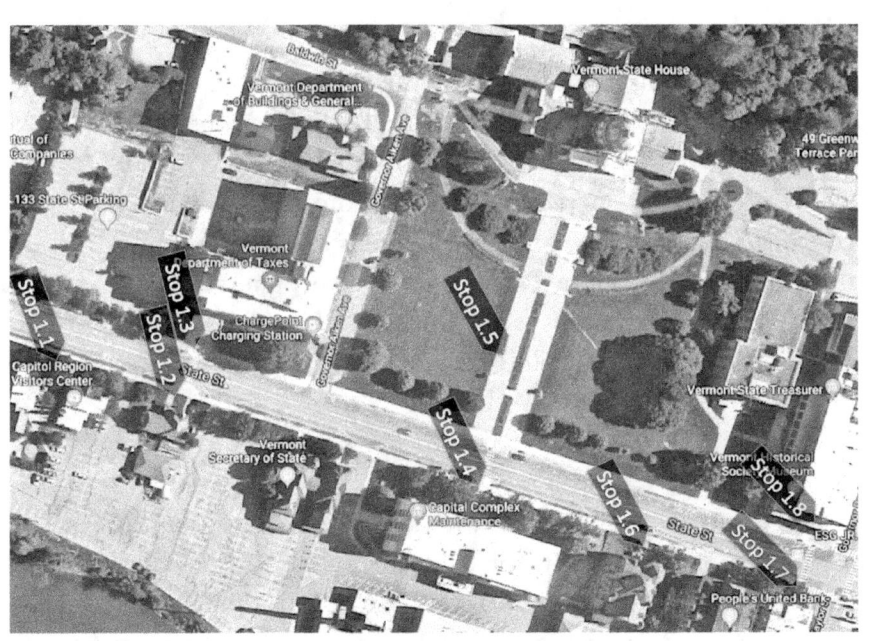

STOP 1.1 - A QUICK HISTORICAL OVERVIEW

VISITORS CENTER - 134 STATE STREET

*I*NTRODUCTION
This tour begins at the Visitors Center at 134 State Street and ends farther up this same street near the Capitol Plaza Hotel. The Visitors Center is open from 6am-5pm M-F, and 9-5 on weekends. It has a spotless public restroom and a water cooler, and coffee is available for a donation. There is a sculpture garden next to the building and you might want to stroll around or sit in that area during this stop, which is a quick historical overview of Montpelier. You could also stay inside the Visitors Center for this part.

EARLIEST DAYS

Going all the way back to the time before Europeans arrived on the continent, there isn't much evidence to help us know who lived in this area prior to the late 1700s, but to tell the truth there haven't been many concerted archeological efforts to find them. There have been a few discoveries of artifacts, though, that suggest Native Americans – particularly the Abenaki tribe - were here at one time, but our first documentation of Montpelier comes when it was formally chartered in 1781, during the period when Vermont had declared itself an independent republic.

Founding Father

A Revolutionary War veteran named Colonel Jacob Davis gets the credit as the city's founder.

He came here from Massachusetts with his wife Rebecca and their sons, and for the first several years Jacob was a regular Paul Bunyan. He cleared land at the rate of an acre a day, according to historical eyewitnesses.

How We Got Our Name

Jacob Davis built the first streets in the town that came to be known as Montpelier. It was named after a city of the same name in France, probably because of the general good feeling toward France as an American ally during the war.

How We Became the State Capital

Through the end of the 18th century, the Legislature convened in spots all over the state because there was no fixed capital for Vermont, but in 1805 the government was officially transferred here because of its central location. It's been the capital ever since, but for a while, we had a hard time hanging on to the title. There was often some sneaky movement afoot to move everything off to Burlington, but Montpelier kept a firm grip and won out in the end.

First known image of Montpelier circa 1821, Sarah Waltrous

Montpelier Today

The city today has a population that moves between 8,000-9,000 people. We are the smallest capital city in the country, and that superlative gives me the excuse to note that we are also the only one without a McDonald's.

Keep that in mind if it ever comes up as a *Jeopardy* question. We like to brag about it, so it isn't likely to change.

In fairness, though, we have only to go a few miles south for our Big Mac fix. And although we have only about 8,000 residents, the population swells daily to as many as 21,000, factoring in all the private and state employees who come here to work, and those who have business to conduct with any of them.

To give you some general perspective on what you'll be seeing during these tours, the city has the largest historic district in the state. Its listing in the National Register of Historic Places has been expanded twice, and now encompasses 533 historic structures.

Welcome to the Neighborhood

If you haven't done so already, head back to the sidewalk in front of the Visitors Center. Here, we're on the northwestern edge of what's known as the "Capitol Complex". Most of the houses you'll see in the next few blocks are state-owned and have various agencies in them, but many date back to the 1800s when this was a fashionable residential neighborhood.

The house adjacent to the Visitor Center's garden is the birthplace and childhood home of US Senator Patrick Leahy. During legislative sessions, his parents Alba and Howard rented rooms to lawmakers and also ran a printing press in the back of the house. It now houses the Vermont Council on the Arts, and through the side entrance you can access the small Spotlight Gallery featuring Vermont artists. Admission is free, and it's open Monday thru Friday from 8:30-4:30.

As we start heading up the street toward the State House, I want you to keep three family names in mind, because amongst the three of them they owned a lot of the property at this end of the street during the 19th century. The names are Taplin, Reed, and Dewey.

STOP 1.2 - A PAINTED LADY

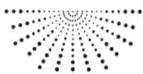

132 STATE STREET

*I*f you were on a mission to visit the State Auditor of Accounts, you probably wouldn't expect to find such a serious-sounding official in this whimsical, dollhouse setting, right? Such is the charm of small capitals and small government.

Notice the steep roof, the covered porches, and all the towers and spindles and froufrou. These are all clues that this house was constructed in a style known as Queen Anne Revival, which was very popular in the country during the late 1800s and early 1900s. The paint job gives it the added distinction of being what's known as a "Painted Lady", a term commonly applied to colorfully repainted Victorian style houses.

FIG. 58. EASTLAKE HOUSE

Off the Beaten Path: If you'd like to see more of this style, you'll find them in some of the residential streets surrounding the downtown area, particularly around Liberty and Loomis Streets. These neighborhoods are quiet, leafy, and picturesque. In them, you'll find a diverse display of architecture, including a few Painted Ladies demurely screening themselves behind flowering trees and foliage.

This particular house that our state auditor occupies originally belonged to the Taplins, which is one of those families I mentioned a minute ago. The Taplins were a big family, and by big I mean they could field a couple of baseball teams. John Taplin, Jr. managed to sire a grand total of…21 children. There is a parenthetical comment in the historical record clarifying that John Jr. did have children by two wives, but I'm not sure that makes anything better for either of them! This house belonged to his son George. He and the rest of the Taplin clan were quite the gang of wheeler-dealer speculators in 19th century Montpelier. Apparently trying to trace their various transactions and deed exchanges produces a tangled cat's cradle of a mess.

Swivel around now and look across the street. The Beaux Arts style building metaphorically looming over our fairytale cottage is commonly known as the Tax Department, but it didn't start out that way. In the next stop, I'll tell you how it got there.

STOP 1.3 - A MOST BEAUTIFUL TAX DEPARTMENT

133 STATE STREET

*T*here's been a lot of activity and a few address changes on this parcel of land over the years. It had two houses on it in the late 1800s which were owned by brothers Charles and George W. Reed. The Reed family was another of the city's early and illustrious dynasties. They were lawyers, businessmen, real estate speculators, public office holders and everything in between. Charles was the State Librarian for many years, and his brother George was the Secretary for the National Life Insurance Company. The Prudential may have grabbed the logo first, but National Life has been Montpelier's very own Rock of Gibraltar for over 150 years. It's got an interesting history that I'll say more about later.

WE'LL STAY HERE FOREVER - OR MAYBE NOT

The company acquired the properties on this plot and financed the construction of the building you see here now. It served as the 6th home office National Life had moved into since it was founded. The other five were scattered along the street here and we'll see a lot of them before we're done. They moved into this building in 1920. As you face it, you might think the design looks a little off balance, and you would not be wrong. If you peek around the left side of the building, you'll see most of that exterior wall is done in a dull yellow brick with no granite facing. It was left this way because the original plan was to put another wing on the left that matched the right when the time came to expand again. This would result in a much larger building with the main entrance serving as a central portico. But it never happened.

Instead of expanding in place, National Life left this building in 1960 for their current headquarters on a hilltop above the city. The State eventually bought the vacated building to house the Tax Department, and I'm sure there's a joke in there somewhere about life and death and taxes.

Montpelier's Moving Houses

You might assume the Reed homes were demolished to make way for this big new building, but that's not the case. In the mid 20th century, demolition would become more common, much to our collective sorrow, but before that Montpelier's town planners often preferred to just move things around. They did it a lot, like the houses on a Monopoly board, and we'll see many examples of that on these tours.

Charles Reed's transported home eventually moldered into a ruin so that is lost to us, but if you wanted to see the original home of his brother George, you could walk a few hundred yards west of this spot and find it at 8 Bailey Avenue.

During business hours the Tax building is open to the public, and the ornate, vaulted ceiling of the lobby just inside the door is worth a quick look.

A Vermont "Character"

In the entrance vestibule, you'll also see a bronze relief of Daniel Leavens Cady, a certifiable Vermont "character". Born in Windsor in 1861, he became a New York City lawyer who retired to Vermont to write poetry. I'm not sure why he came to be memorialized in this way, but as you can see from the bronze likeness he was said to never be without his top hat, and stories have it that he was also something of a humorist who liked a drink or two now and then.

More Sliding Buildings

Our next destination is the area in front of the State House. For now, stay on the even-numbered side of the street and have a look at the houses at numbers 128 and 126 State Street as we pass them. Both are also done in the Queen Anne Revival style. 128 is the office of the Secretary of State. It was originally owned by Edward Dewey, a member of a very important family in the development of Montpelier through the 19th century. More to come about them, but for now I just wanted to mention that this big, complicated looking brick house is another example of one that was moved from its original location farther up the street.

The photos taken of the process show the house jacked up off the ground as if it weighed no more than a paper maché model. The house beside it is another Painted Lady and the American Legion has its state headquarters office inside. Don't look for a bar in there because there isn't one, but if you're a member, the Post 3 lodge is on Main Street. Now let's move on, and we'll stop next in front of the large marble-faced office building up ahead.

STOP 1.4 - A COUNTRY DOCTOR AND A HOMETOWN HERO

120 STATE STREET

*I*f you're facing the State House, the first thing I'm going to ask is that you turn around and face the building behind you, which is simply called the State Office Building. More informally, it's called the DMV – the Department of Motor Vehicles. Like DMVs around the country, the building conjures visions of purgatory, but I kid you not – anyone I've ever encountered there has been friendly and polite, as are most state employees. And I'd say that even if I wasn't one myself!

Our DMV is Art Deco Baby!

That brick house we just saw originally sat on this piece of land. Once it was moved, along with a few other houses, this Art Deco behemoth of concrete and steel started going up and was completed in 1949. It's faced on all sides with Vermont marble. If you look up near the roofline, you can see an engraved frieze surrounding the building that includes the name of each of the state's 14 counties. The figure carved in relief on the steel front door is Ceres, the Roman goddess of agriculture and fertility. She is holding the Vermont state seal in one hand, and beneath her is the iconic image of a man attaching a sap bucket to his maple tree. I know the building looks sort of like a giant mausoleum, but never mind that! If you walk through the big steel door, inside you'll see a plaque on the wall to the right marking it as the spot – THE VERY SPOT!! – where George Dewey, Admiral of the Navy and Victor of Manila Bay, was born. This brings us to the third illustrious family that I mentioned earlier, so have a seat on the wall while I tell you their story.

The Country Doctor With A Vision

Dr. Julius Yemans Dewey was born in 1801 in Berlin. He got his medical degree at the University of Vermont and then set up a practice in Montpelier. In 1848 he got together a Board of Directors and formed the National Life Insurance Company.

As president and chief medical officer, Dr. Dewey rode around on horseback selling policies all over Vermont and as far north as Montreal. It was very efficient, one-stop shopping when he arrived at your door because he would do the medical exam, approve the case and issue your policy on the spot.

Everything was going great…until they got their first claim in 1850. One of the company's first policies went to a healthy 22-year old fellow from Ferrisburg, which seemed like a safe bet, but he left Vermont to join the Gold Rush "Forty Niners" who were sailing off to California, and died of dysentery in San Diego before he'd even left the ship. This presented a big problem for National Life because they didn't have enough money to pay the claim. They'd only been in business for a little over a year. But the Directors chipped in and somehow scraped together the thousand dollars, and in a stroke of PR genius Dr. Dewey personally delivered the cash to the deceased man's young widow only 3 days after receiving the claim. Public accolades and glowing media coverage followed and the company was on its way.

It's first office was in Dr. Dewey's quaint gingerbread-style home which was also on this site and also got moved farther down State

Street. Unfortunately, it did not survive the 1960s, which was the beginning of the dark demolition years in Montpelier.

The Doctor's Son Takes to The Sea

I'll finish up with the Deweys by returning to our hero Admiral George, the son of Julius. He apparently started with the heroic antics at a young age because it's said he used to run up and down the State House steps blindfolded. He went to the Norwich Military School, now Norwich University, which is 10 miles south of here, then graduated from the Naval Academy and went to sea. He served on a steam-paddle frigate during the Civil War and continued to move up in rank over the years. It was a thoroughly respectable, not especially exciting career. He was even a lighthouse inspector for several years. Then came the Spanish American War.

The Hero of Manila Bay

I won't try to sort out the details for why this war happened at all, but George Dewey was promoted to the rank of Commodore and in 1898 took command of the Asiatic squadron. War was declared, and the squadron steamed to the Spanish-occupied Philippines and into Manila Bay. On May 1, Dewey, on board the *USS Olympia*, immortalized the ship's captain Vernon Gridley with the line "You may fire when ready, Gridley".

Original painting hangs in the State House

Well. Six hours later, the entire Spanish fleet was at the bottom of Manila Bay, with no loss of American life, and George Dewey was an instant American hero.

Let me tell you, the reaction was complete, nationwide Deweymania. When he got back to Washington, Congress first made him a rear Admiral, then one-upped themselves by inventing the rank of Admiral of the Navy and they gave him that title as well. No one has ever held the rank since. They also gave him a house. A special military medal was struck with his face on it and produced by Tiffany. Then Congress gave Tiffany $10,000 more to produce a custom-made sword which was presented to Dewey by President McKinley. Then he started on a triumphal tour of the country. In New York the parade took two days to finish. In Boston 280 members of the Handel & Haydn Society sang *Hail the Conquering Hero Comes* as he arrived at City Hall.

People started naming children, dogs, streets and schools after him. The super cool catch-phrase of the day was "you may fire when ready, Gridley."

He might have been America's first massive media celebrity.

Dewey Day in Montpelier

Finally, he had a Vermont homecoming, which the state had been planning for 2 months before his arrival. Dewey made his way through Vermont by train, and after stops along the way and a 17-gun salute, he got to Montpelier to find every building draped in bunting, and his face in electric lights hanging on the front of the State House.

Special railway tracks were constructed to bring all the people into town for the celebration. There were grandstands built along the streets for the parade, and on Dewey Day itself, as the Admiral cruised through his hometown in a horse-drawn carriage, an estimated 40,000 people crammed the sidelines screaming themselves hoarse.

There were thousands of pounds of fireworks set off that night in a nearby meadow, and to top it all an enormous bonfire was lit on the hill behind the State House, which at the time had no trees on it.

It was quite simply the biggest thing that had ever happened in Vermont and certainly in its capital city. It's exhausting to even describe! Imagine what it must have been like to experience it! Well, we in Montpelier were lucky enough to get a taste of it in 1999 when (shameless plug, here) my father, Paul H Guare, encouraged the city to mark the centennial of Dewey Day with another celebration. I don't know if it was as big as the original, but it was certainly the largest faithfully executed historical reenactment the city ever put on. We even had a Navy veteran playing the role of Dewey, and he was the spitting image of the Admiral.

Now, let's cross the street for a closer look at the State House.

STOP 1.5 - FLOODS, FIRES AND GODDESSES

STATE HOUSE MAIN PROMENADE

If you're walking along the State House promenade any time between May and October, you'll probably marvel – as I always do – at the beautifully maintained gardens and lawn. This is essentially Montpelier's Central Park and it gets a lot of use throughout the year. Naturally it's a gathering spot for protests, but it's just as often a place of celebration and leisure. There's many an ultimate Frisbee match played on the lawns in the summer, and in recent years we've added a skating rink in the winter.

The Great Flood of 1927

As you're walking up the promenade, you'll see a plaque on the right-hand granite post that marks the high-water mark for the massive flood in November 1927 that decimated all of the downtown area. More than 8 inches of rain fell over a period of 48 hours, and at its peak, the water rose to a height of 12 feet at the intersection of State and Main Streets. When the water receded only one road of a dozen out of town was passable, and only 7 of the city's 24 bridges were undamaged. Almost every building in the downtown area was either destroyed or heavily damaged. Sitting at the confluence of two rivers – the Winooski and the North Branch, the city itself is a flood plain, so it's seen plenty of high water over the years since, but all of them are measured against the Flood of '27, and the devastation of that one has thankfully never been equaled.

State House Construction - 3rd Time's the Charm

As it is set on a hill, the State House escaped damage during the 1927 flood. The current building is the third on this site. The first was a very humble wooden building put up in the time of Jacob Davis, after Montpelier became the capital. The legend is that the rough and tumble farming legislators who came to town for the winter literally whittled it into a ruin.

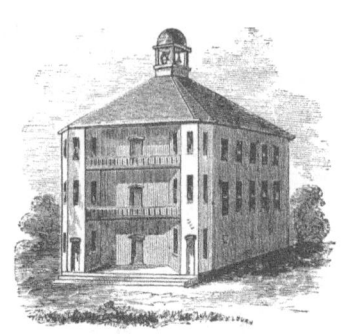

A second one was built between 1833-38 and looked more like the one you see today, although it had a lower, saucer-style copper dome that looked a bit like the Jefferson memorial in Washington.

It was constructed from granite brought from a quarry in Barre about twelve miles away. The loads were transported on wagons, each drawn by four horses and a yoke of oxen.

That version didn't last very long, either. In January 1857, after the boilers in the basement had been running at full steam over several days of frigid weather, some beams above the boiler overheated and started a fire that destroyed the building. All that remained was the portico and Doric columns and a few of the surrounding granite walls.

The third and present structure incorporated the portico, and the discoloration you see in the columns is a result of that 1857 fire. The new wooden dome was done more in the style of the nation's capital, and was originally painted a dark red. It wasn't gilded until the early 20th century.

Ceres the Beloved

The statue on top is not a historical figure, it's a goddess. Ceres the goddess of agriculture, and we've had three of them atop the dome over the years. The original was carved from Vermont pine and installed as part of the 1858 construction, but unfortunately the goddess rotted away and fell into pieces when it was removed in 1938. The Sergeant at Arms at the time was a man named Dwight Dwinell, and although he wasn't a trained sculptor he agreed to have a go at carving a replacement from Ponderosa pine, which was supposed to be harder than the Vermont version. The result was a lovely piece of folk art rather than a more classically polished piece, but we loved it, and at such a height it was hard to pick out the flaws anyway. It turned out Ponderosa Pine isn't much hardier than the Vermont variety. It lasted until the spring of 2018, when once again the weather-soaked goddess was delicately lifted from the dome, in one piece this time.

The latest version of Ceres has been carved from Honduran mahogany for maximum durability. While the artist, Chris Miller, was working on the project, the dome also underwent major renovations and re-gilding. It would be hard to overstate how beloved Ceres is in the local psyche. When she returned in November 2018 there were over a thousand people here to celebrate as a giant crane floated her into place. A delightful fun story: As a tribute to our popular and very dedicated State House Curator David Schutz, the artist is said to have carved a small likeness of his face on the back of the statue, amongst the sheaves of wheat. Complete with trademark bow tie.

Vermont Supreme Court And Art Gallery

As you're approaching the steps of the State House, note the granite building to your right. That's Vermont's Supreme Court building. It was completed in 1918.

Before that, the court officially met in the State House, but it got so crowded that the justices were often chivvied over to a room in the Pavilion Hotel for their deliberations. In the lobby of the Supreme Court building there is a changing art exhibit that is free and open to the public.

When you reach the third level on your way up the steps, you might want to detour off to the right or left for a look at the cannons. They are relics of the Spanish American War, taken from one of the ships that hometown hero Admiral George Dewey helped send to the bottom of Manila Bay. Kids love to climb on them – I know I always did – and it is fine to let them do so.

The Battle of Bennington - You Owe Us One!

On the portico itself, to one side there is a statue depicting Ethan Allen, one of Vermont's founding fathers and a Revolutionary War hero who led his Green Mountain Boys in the capture of Fort Ticonderoga. On the other side is a cannon captured by General John Stark at the Battle of Bennington in 1777.

Bennington Battle Day on August 16 is an official holiday unique to Vermont when all state offices are closed. I once thought we were making more of it than it deserved, until I did the research.

It turns out the Vermont militia delivered such a blow to the British army at that battle that it was a major factor leading to General Burgoyne's eventual surrender at Saratoga, which prompted France to enter the war as an American ally, which definitively turned the tide, and the rest is history.

So, you're welcome. We'll take the day off for that, thank you very much.

Touring the State House Interior

I will leave you here at the door to explore the interior of the State House on your own. This is a visit not to be missed. It is a piece of living history – a beautiful, lovingly preserved gem that looks mostly how it did when it was built. There's no admission charge. There are self-guided tours you can operate with your smartphone, or you can get a printed version, and at times volunteers are available for guided tours. The hours are Monday-Friday from 7:45-4:15, and from July to October it's also open from 11-3 on Saturdays. There are restrooms inside and a cafeteria that is usually open on weekdays.

Off the Beaten Path: If you're visiting during the winter, there's a tradition called Farmer's Night, dating back to when the legislators were often farmers who came to town for the week. The Legislature is still only officially scheduled to be in session from January to April, a holdover from the time when the farmers had to get back home for the spring planting. Each Wednesday evening during that period, there is a concert or some other form of entertainment staged in the House of Representatives with the audience sitting in the legislators' chairs. It is free to lawmakers and the public alike, and it keeps the representatives from whittling at the walls of our capitol building.

I will meet you back on the sidewalk of State Street at the foot of the steps of the Department of Agriculture, which is that big castle-like building across the street, to the left of the State Office building.

STOP 1.6 - ON THE EDGE OF WHERE PRIVATE LIFE BEGINS

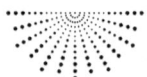

116 STATE STREET

*H*ere at the Department of Agriculture we are close to the eastern edge of the Capitol Complex and in front of one of the most unusual looking buildings on the street. It's done in a style called Richardsonian Romanesque, the most famous example of which is Trinity Church in Copley Square, Boston. It's maybe a bit disappointing to hear it wasn't once the fabulous mansion of a Montpelier millionaire. It was just one of the headquarters buildings that National Life moved into and grew out of. This one was particularly special though, because its original interior was a marvelous mixture of mahogany, Egyptian mosaic tiles and marble. It also featured one of Vermont's first elevators. It was kept in use until 1981, much to the terror of any state worker who had to use it. Some of all that good stuff is still visible, although it's been chopped up quite a bit to fit more offices.

The Tragic Demise of Our Train Station

We'll walk a little further on, past the People's United Bank, which is the spot where once stood a majestic train station with a clock tower. It was built in 1880 and brought down with the help of dynamite in 1963. One Vermont historian categorized its destruction as nothing short of an act of vandalism. There is a heartbreaking photo of the explosion, with the beautiful clocktower looking like a laser-guided missile had just slammed into it. It's a blunt force signal that the genteel age of trundling old buildings to new locations had finished and an age of demolition had begun.

STOP 1.7 - THE KEELEY CURE

110 STATE STREET

*A*fter the bank is 110 State Street. Before it moved two doors down, National Life also lived here for a while as a tenant of the Vermont Mutual Fire Insurance Company, which owned the building. But it is more interesting as the one-time home for the Montpelier branch of a substance abuse treatment franchise called the Keeley Institute. It rented space in the building from 1892-95. This was a time when opium was sold over the counter, making opiate addiction and alcoholism as endemic in the late 19th century as it is today. Founded in Illinois, the Keeley Institute was one of the first to address the scourge as a disease rather than a moral issue and was known to create a supportive and caring environment for its patients.

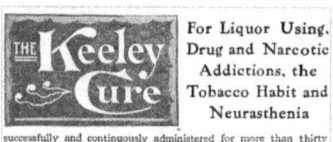

Its treatment regimen may have been questionable, though. It required the administration of injections its founder called "bichloride of gold", but he refused to ever disclose what the actual ingredients were. Patients were also supplied with as much whiskey as they cared to drink until voluntarily giving it up. Business took off like a rocket as Montpelier's citizens embraced the treatment with enthusiasm. There was very little privacy involved, either. Newspapers around the state sprinkled in announcements of treatments much as they did the births and vacation plans of their citizens, and many treatment graduates went public to testify to their success in conquering their addiction.

Eventually, the Institute came under attack from competing recovery centers, and the Montpelier franchise in particular was beset with rumors of embezzlement. It closed in 1895, but by then over 500 patients were said to have taken the "Keeley Cure" during its short life-span in the building. For a while it was a trendy destination for the wealthy. While taking their treatments, they could enjoy the amenities of the capital city while comfortably installed in the state's finest grand hotel right across the street, which is where we will turn our attention next.

STOP 1.8 - THE GRAND OLD LADY

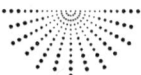

109 STATE STREET

*H*ere at the edge of the hurly burly of Montpelier's commercial life, we come to a building that perfectly captures the balance between the city as seat of government and a bustling area of private commerce. During its heyday, the Pavilion Hotel sheltered not only private visitors from all over the world but also many of the part-time state representatives who came to town for Legislative sessions. After the House and Senate, the Pavilion was sometimes referred to as "Vermont's Third House".

BUILD IT AND THEY WILL COME

The origins of a hotel on this site began with Thomas Davis, the son of Jacob. By the time he was an adult, Montpelier had been the capital for a few years, the first state house was up and running and Tom shrewdly understood the legislators and their supplicants (we call them lobbyists now) were going to need a place to stay, and that if he built it they would come. So he put up a structure on this spot and called it the Davis Tavern. And they came. There is some speculation that the Marquis de Lafayette was entertained at the tavern during his stay in Montpelier – although there is a plaque downtown insisting that he spent the night in a house on Main Street.

A HOTEL FOR PRESIDENTS AND FILM STARS

The tavern changed hands a few times and at some point its name was changed to the Pavilion. When it was sold again in 1874, the owner promptly tore the building down and in its place erected a modern, 90-room luxury hotel. It was designed in a style called "Steamboat Gothic", with double decker wraparound verandahs. The hotel continued to be popular with those involved with the government, but it also became a popular summer destination for visitors from Boston and New York, who arrived by train at the elegant train station across the street.

Over the years additional rooms were added, along with an elevator and state-of-the-art plumbing. By the turn of the century it was known as one of the finest hotels in New England. It hosted four different presidents during its glory years – Theodore Roosevelt, Taft, Hoover and of course Vermont native Calvin Coolidge. It even had a visit from Alfred Hitchcock and Shirley MacLaine when they were in Vermont to film *The Trouble With Harry*.

Everything Old is New Again

Of course by the 1960s times had changed. People were traveling more by car instead of train, and our nice train station was gone anyway. (Can you tell I'm bitter about that?) The Pavilion fell on hard times and closed its doors for good in 1966. Now, what to do? A battle royal ensued for the next four years. Office space was at a premium in the Capitol Complex, so there was a strong argument on one side for demolition to make way for a modern office building. On the other side an equally tenacious group argued in favor of preservation. The Legislature was divided. The question dragged on. What do you think happened in the end?

Yeah, they tore it down. But the story has a happier ending than that! The Pizzagalli Construction Company saved the day with the creative solution of designing an entirely modern building that identically reproduced the façade of the old hotel. Modern materials and technology were used, but the bricks were made from 19th century molds, and some of the original pieces were re-used – verandah spindles, granite sills and keystones. Inside the place is crammed with state offices, and the governor's working office is on the top floor.

The only portion of the interior that was created to identically reproduce the original is the Victorian Lounge, which is to the left after you enter the front door. So the historical building you see you before you today is a little bit of a hoax, but we'll take it, because you only have to look at our post office to realize it could have been much, much worse.

VISITING THE VERMONT HISTORICAL SOCIETY MUSEUM

Another bonus is that we got the wonderful Vermont Historical Society Museum out of the deal, which occupies the ground floor of the building and is another must see attraction. It's usually open from 10-4, Tuesdays through Saturdays, and there is an admission charge that is well worth it. You'll want to plan on about 60 to 90 minutes for your visit.

Eat, Drink and Shop

And now you've seen the Capitol Complex! Is it time to eat yet?! There aren't many options at the lower end of State Street other than possibly the State House cafeteria, but from this point forward there are lots of options. If you want a super quick, easy take-away, the **Capital Deli** and convenience store right here at State and Taylor makes sandwiches to order. For restaurants, you'll find something for everyone at **J. Morgans** in the Capitol Plaza Hotel because their menu is enormous. Across the street, **Pho Capital** is a great and very reasonably priced Vietnamese restaurant that also does takeout and it's in a historic building that I discuss in Tour 2. There are lots more further downtown that I'll cover in Tour 2, which I hope you'll join me for next!

TOUR 2 - THE SHOPPING DISTRICT

A GHOST STORY AND AN INVISIBLE BRIDGE

STOP 2.1 - THE CAPITOL PLAZA'S ANCESTORS

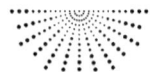

100 STATE STREET

*I*ntroduction
Hello and welcome back! This is Tour #2, which begins outside the main entrance of the Capitol Plaza Hotel and ends at the intersection of State and Main. We'll be walking through the main shopping district, so along with a little history, I'll be giving you the low-down on stores and restaurants you might want to check out during your visit. If you're ready, let's get started!

"Montpelier House"

Montpelier has some lovely inns and B&Bs, but the Capitol Plaza in its present and earlier design has been the only traditional, full-service hotel in the city for decades. The block it sits on has been the home of hotels for almost 200 years, and the way it's changed over the years in some ways reflects how transportation itself evolved in the 18th and 19th centuries.

There was a sprawling wood-framed place called Montpelier House on this site in the 1820s, and photographs on view in City Hall show an open archway in the middle that was tall and wide enough to drive a stagecoach through it.

Which sounds romantic, right? Well it was a pretty miserable trip over bumpy, muddy roads, but it was the only way to get here until the railroad arrived in 1849. In the early 1880s two train depots stood at opposite ends of town. The tracks ran right behind the hotel, and when Montpelier later started a trolley car service, there were tracks running by the front door as well. The trolley line stretched from lower State Street to Main, then took a right and trundled along all the way to Barre, branching out to a few other neighborhoods along the way. The flood of 1927 that was so catastrophic to Montpelier wiped out the trolley, and it never really recovered, but by then Henry Ford was putting cars on the road by the million, so one way or another its fate was sealed.

A Hotel for the Motor Age

The Pavilion Hotel that we talked about in the first tour had flourished during the railroad days, but it floundered during the automobile age.

While it was beginning a slow, long decline, over here on this block the new owners were seizing the moment. A no-frills rectangular brick building went up in

1932, the hotel was rechristened the Montpelier Tavern, and postcards from that time pointedly included a car parked right in front of the grand colonnaded entrance.

As if that didn't "drive" the point home, they changed the name again in the 1960s to the Tavern Motor Inn. They also opened a split-level lounge called the "Justin Morgan Room" after the famous Vermonter who established the Morgan horse breed. With its red leatherette furniture and horse-head décor, it was a real "Mad Men" style watering hole for the movers and shakers in town.

As J. Morgan's it has a more contemporary vibe. If you take advantage of their Sunday brunch buffet, when you load up your plate you will be standing on the site of the Motor Inn's old swimming pool.

The City's First Buildings

From this spot, we have a view of some of the oldest buildings that formed the core of early Montpelier. This is where things began taking shape in the 1780s, when town founder Jacob Davis got busy with the lumberjacking. The brick Vermont Federal building across the street was built in 1816, the wooden clapboard one to the right of it was built in 1810. To the left of the Vermont Federal building, set back from the street, is another structure from the same era. Right now, it's a Vietnamese restaurant called Pho Capital, but old-timers sometimes still refer to this building as "The Thrush". That's because it operated for many years as the Thrush Tavern, named after the Vermont State Bird. It was a place of low-lit nooks and crannies and another popular spot where many a legislative logjam was eased with the help of a few stiff drinks. In Tour #1 we talked a lot about buildings moving around and this is another one. It originally sat close to the street, in line with those next to it, but it got moved back to make way for a gas station, which has since been torn down.

Capitol Theater - Art Deco Grandeur

Our next stop is about 100 yards up the street, in front of the Christ Episcopal Church, where you can sit on a bench if you like, and look at several things at once while I tell their stories. As you pass it, take note of our fabulous, Art Deco Capitol Theater, which is one of the most photographed buildings in town after the State House. It still has its original green-glazed brickwork and neon-lit marquee. Its gala opening in 1939 featured the world premiere of "Rulers of the Sea" starring the young and very handsome Douglas Fairbanks Jr. The space has been updated from one big theater with a balcony to many smaller theaters, but the original ticket booth and candy counter are both still in operation, and there are some lingering vestiges of its red formica splendor.

STOP 2.2 - A MURDER AND A GHOST STORY

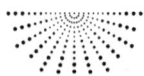

65 STATE STREET, COUNTY COURTHOUSE

The best vantage point for viewing the Montpelier County Courthouse is the pocket park of the Christ Episcopal Church across the street from it, which gets very active in the summertime. Also, if you are here on a Saturday morning in summer or fall, you may now be wading into the heart of the Capital City Farmers Market. It's a vibrant presence in this neighborhood each weekend from 10am-2pm. For years it was exclusively in the long, wide parking lot next to the church, but there are ongoing experiments to close part of State Street for vendors, so by the time you are listening to this, I'm not sure which place they'll be in, but you shouldn't have any trouble finding them.

We'll talk more about the church in a bit, but first have a look across the street at our courthouse.

COUNTY COURTHOUSE - ANOTHER 3-TIME CHARMER

We talked about the earlier, Jeffersonian version of the State House that was destroyed by fire, and unfortunately that was not an unusual occurrence in 19th century Montpelier. There aren't many buildings from that era we can talk about without adding "and then it burned."

One example is this courthouse. The one you see now is essentially the third one on this site. The first, made of brick, was built in 1843 and burned down practically before the paint was dry. It was replaced with another brick building, which also had a major fire in 1880, but that one left enough of the outside walls standing to rebuild it into the Greek Revival structure you see today.

Hell Hath No Fury...

The courthouse has of course seen a lot of drama over the years, and one of the more sensational cases was an 1898 murder trial that provides the origin for two separate ghost stories. Mildred Brewster was the bored and restless daughter of a wealthy farmer from Huntington. She came to Montpelier looking for excitement when she was 21, and got more than she bargained for. She fell in love with Jack Wheeler, a handsome granite worker living in the same boarding house with her. The problem was that Jack had already fallen in love with a local girl named Anna, and he was entirely devoted to her. *Or was he?* He is said to have admitted being intimate with Mildred, but then became engaged to Anna, and Mildred was having none of it.

She bought a $3 revolver in Barre, spent a few hours in the fields above Montpelier practicing her aim, and the following day – a rainy Memorial Day – she invited Anna out for a walk on Seminary Hill, the site of the present-day Vermont College of Fine Arts. Witnesses report seeing them walk out under the same umbrella toward Jack's house, which was nearby on Sibley Avenue. A few minutes later, Mildred drew her gun, fired a shot directly into Anna's head, and another shot into her own. Mildred survived; Anna did not.

The murder trial was an internationally reported sensation, and it was standing room only in this county courthouse a year later, when Mildred was declared not guilty by reason of insanity. She spent the rest of her life at the Waterbury State Asylum for the Insane, but is said to be spending her after-life in the halls of the county courthouse. Staff over the years have reported sounds of glass shattering, items out of place, and voices in empty rooms.

VCFA College Hall

Meanwhile, up at the main hall of the College of Fine Arts, there have also been reports over many years of glass breaking, doors closing and pictures falling off the walls in unison. They are attributed to the murdered Anna, who is said to be haunting the tower of College Hall.

VCFA's ghost is regarded with such fondness that the college named its café after her.

Off the Beaten Path: With or without ghosts, Café Anna is a lovely place to stop for a morning cup of coffee. Its hours are Monday through Friday from 8:30 am to 1:30 pm, with expanded hours during student residencies throughout the year. To reach the college from this spot, go up State Street to the main intersection with Main, cross straight over to East State Street and up to the top of what was once called Seminary Hill. College Hall also has a bookstore featuring the works of faculty and graduates of the school's writing program.

The street running next to the Courthouse is Elm Street and not too far past the courthouse is the site of Montpelier's first log cabin settlement – this is where Jacob and Rebecca Davis and their sons lived when they first arrived and got busy clearing the wilderness. For future reference, the corner of Elm and State is the starting point for Tour #3 in this series, when we'll talk more about that site.

It Seemed a Good Idea at the Time

To the left of the Courthouse is the Federal Building and Post Office. It stands on the site of an 1891 Romanesque Chateau-style post office constructed from granite and marble that was demolished in 1963. Many local history buffs consider it to be one of the greatest architectural crimes in the city's history, and personally I think they have a point. I challenge anyone to look at a photo of the original, gorgeous building that once stood there without a gasp of dismay.

One interesting feature of the present building, though, which was dedicated in 1964, is the attractive stone facing of the building's ground floor. It is often mistaken for marble, but in fact it is a dark green stone called serpentine. It is pretty rare, so if you see this particular type of stone anywhere else, there's a good chance it is Vermont Verde Antique, which comes from a quarry in Rochester, VT that's been in operation for over 100 years. Another item of interest - the post office is the site of what might be the state's longest anti-war protest. Sponsored by the American Friends Service Committee, more commonly known as Quakers, it has been taking place every Friday at noon in every kind of weather for almost 20 years.

Now, let's turn around and have a closer look at Christ Church.

STOP 2.3 - A GREEN SPACE FOR EVERYONE

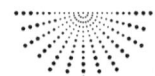

64 STATE STREET, CHRIST CHURCH

The courtyard/pocket park next to Christ Episcopal Church underwent a major renovation in recent years and has become a favorite gathering spot in the city. During August and September there are noontime concerts here every Thursday, and during the other seasons throughout the year the church often features noontime music inside in the sanctuary.

The Gothic-style church was built from Vermont granite in 1868, and the parish house annex at the end of the courtyard was added later. Originally, the tower had a steeple on top of it, but between a major fire, and then the devastating flood of 1927, it became destabilized and was eventually removed in 1963. The lovely interior has a Gothic vaulted ceiling and rose window and is well worth a look if the church is open.

There is a green space on the other side of the church as well. It's called the Ralph Geer Memorial Garden. Since it's designed to be a sacred, meditative space the gate is usually locked, but if the parish house office is open you can ask for permission to go inside.

STOP 2.4 - AN INVISIBLE BRIDGE

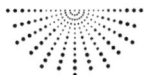

41-45 STATE STREET

Before leaving the intersection of Elm and State Streets, have a look at the Court House's opposite corner. Back in 1861 a wooden building stood near this site that served as the post office. Where did it go? Down the street and around the corner.

You can see for yourself where it shuffled off to, because it is still coyly hiding away in Pitkin Court behind the fire station on Main Street. It was built by James G. French, a successful Montpelier clothing merchant. He also served as postmaster and got into construction in a big way in the latter half of the 19th century. You'll hear his name a few more times on these tours.

Another James you'll be hearing about is James R. Langdon, also a very important figure in the commercial life of Montpelier in the late 19th century. He put up the current building in 1874, and it originally had a flat roof. The decorative mansard roof and round dormers seen now were added about 20 years later. Along with the post office, the main tenant was a bank that remained there under different names for well over a hundred years. The place is still often called the Chittenden Bank Building because nobody gave it a different name. The bank's vault has been creatively incorporated into the interior atmosphere for several businesses that moved in when the bank finally left.

RIALTO ON THE NORTH BRANCH

Walking past it, you'll come next to the Rialto Bridge. It was built in 1915 and is probably the most unusual of its kind in Vermont, because most of it is invisible. It's made of steel I-beams encased in concrete, and has a width of 70 feet, the longest span of its kind in the state. It takes its name from the structure built on top of it. If you turn and look across the street you'll see the Rialto Block, with its name over the doorway. The best perspective on this unusual bridge is from the truss-style steel bridge you can see upriver on Langdon Street (which, yes, is named after James Langdon, or more accurately, he named the street after himself when he created it). From there, you can watch the waters of the North Branch disappear under the Rialto – both bridge and building - and stream out the other side.

On the Rialto bridge as you are facing the river, you'll see a sign on the side of the Chittenden Bank building to the left. It is offering to sell the air rights over the river to build a deck connecting one building to the other, and there's a story behind that.

The sign was posted by Jeff Jacobs, a famous and controversial figure in Montpelier's real estate community for several decades. In 1996 he filed a permit to put a McDonald's in the bank building, which he owned. The idea did not go over well. The permit was rejected by the City Council, not least for the fact that it would have required installing a 3-story fryer vent on the side of the historic structure. There were lawsuits and appeals, all unsuccessful, and at some point in all the drama this sign appeared. Whether Jacobs actually owns the airspace, or whether it could legally be sold or leased for development, remains an unsettled question, and to most of us it seems best that it remain so.

STOP 2.5 - STATE STREET EATERIES

STATE STREET, BETWEEN ELM AND MAIN

*W*hile we're here on the bridge I'll just take a minute to talk about some of the great stuff you can eat and drink in this vicinity. If you aren't hungry yet, you can skip this part and come back to it later.

In the Chittenden Bank building, the **North Branch Café** is a wonderfully cozy, quiet space for a cup of the best brewed tea you'll ever taste, and it also has the city's only "enomatic machine" which dispenses wine by the ounce.

On the other side of the bridge, **Capitol Grounds** is its perfect complement. It roasts its own coffee beans and has been a fixture in town for years. Up at 6am looking for your first cup of joe? You'll find it in all strengths here, along with various things to nosh.

Next door, **Alla Vita** offers a heavenly assortment of olive oils and vinegars, which you can sample to your heart's content. It also offers takeout lunches from a counter in the rear.

Across the street, **Julio's Cantina** has all your Mexican favorites and is open for lunch and dinner, with some great outdoor seating.

Kismet next door is a great choice for weekend brunch indoors or out. It's open for dinner Wednesdays-Saturday with an ever-changing excellent menu and a fabulous cocktail bar. On Tuesday evenings, one of the chefs hosts a cash-only pop-up called Double King, offering an eclectic Chinese tasting menu.

A little farther down is the tiny, hugely popular **Wilaiwan Kitchen**, offering authentic Thai cuisine. It's open weekdays for lunch only and often has a line out the door.

Right next to it, you can cool off from all the spicy goodness with some gelato from **Chill**. They have both traditional flavors and some bold non-traditional ones, all available for tasting.

For a sandwich to-go there is a **Subway**, and a little further down the ever-popular **Pinky's**, a favorite of city and state workers alike with a board full of mouth-watering sandwich varieties as well as daily soup specials.

At **Positive Pie**, pizza is just the beginning. The restaurant has a great long bar and full menu, but if you just want a quick slice, you can get that from a counter in the rear and either take it out or eat it there. During the summer they also offer outside seating that's great for people watching.

You aren't done without a little chocolate, right?! Head to the **Cocoa Bean** and try their handmade truffles, turtles, bark and more. For some additional variety in your sweets, or just because more is always better, move on to **Delish** closer to the intersection with Main and State for a festival of jellies, gummies, chocolates and more dispensed in bulk or packaged.

That's a lot of food all within sight of this bridge, so if you need some nourishment, take a break, then meet me back here and we'll continue on.

There are also some shops in this area you shouldn't miss – **Salaam Boutique** provides a colorful line of hand-sewn clothing in

European fabrics. **The Book Garden** has an eclectic collection of graphic novels and vintage comic books. **Woodbury Mountain Toys** is wonderland of toys and games, and **Capital Kitchen** is a wonderland of the culinary variety. There's more of everything further down the so let's get back on the road.

STOP 2.6 - LET'S TALK ABOUT BLOCKS

17 STATE STREET (AND THEREABOUTS)

*P*assing Capitol Grounds and Alla Vita we're moving into the main commercial area of the city and we need to start thinking in terms of blocks. It is the large brick blocks of buildings that were built in the late 19th and early 20th century that give Montpelier its overall air of coherence and character. The blocks are sometimes hard to distinguish when you are browsing among the shops and restaurants along the street, but if you look up to the roof lines you'll get a better idea of where one stops and another begins. The largest on State street is the Union Block, which has an impressive arched granite doorway topped with a decorative iron railing.

A Renewed Interest in Preservation

On the opposite side of the street if you look up you'll see a rooftop pediment identifying the Walton Block. I mentioned earlier that the 60s marked a period when demolition replaced the earlier fashion of moving buildings from one place to another, but the 1967 renovation of the Walton Block was the first to reflect a renewed commitment to historic preservation in the city. All the stamped sheet metal ornamentation on the façade was retained, as well as the 8 columns running along the ground floor, which are made of cast iron.

FIRES AND MORE FIRES!

There's a story to how some of these long city blocks were created, and it's another one that starts with fire – two of them this time. The first was in March 1875. It took down several buildings on Main and State streets, including the original Rialto block we passed earlier. The second and more catastrophic fire was only two months later. Fanned by strong winds, it raged along both sides of Main Street and burned many buildings at the lower end of Barre Street as well. Miraculously, there were no lives lost in either fire.

Our fire chief at the time was a Civil War veteran with the fabulous name of Colonel Perley Pitkin. He had a team of men that he assigned to lead efforts to contain the fire at various points along the street. Many were fellow Civil War veterans and also ministers of the various churches in Montpelier. They are credited with preventing an even wider disaster, using nothing more protective than wet carpets to wrap themselves in while they beat back the flames. By the end of it, such was the destruction that a citizen could stand on the Rialto bridge and have an unobstructed view across town to the area on Barre Street where Sarducci's restaurant is now.

The rebuilding began immediately, and this time the merchants and architects of Montpelier went in for solid, flat-topped brick structures over the more flammable wooden ones with gables and pitched roofs. Most of the large blocks along Main Street were constructed during this period.

Another direct result of these fires was the installation of the city's main water system, including hydrant hook-ups. Berlin Pond, a few miles from the city center was identified as the suitable source. The engineer for the project was a man named Joel Foster, and his publicly-funded memorial can be seen in Green Mount Cemetery today, which is at the lower end of State Street. It is a full-size granite likeness of the man, with a bowler hat in one hand, and his other resting on top of a fire hydrant.

STOP 2.7 - CROSSROADS OF THE CAPITAL

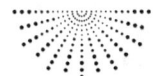

STATE AND MAIN

We've arrived now at the center of town. For this section of the tour, you can stand where the granite-columned TD Bank building wraps itself around the corner, or grab a seat on one of the benches on its State Street side.

WE LOVE A PARADE

We are at the spot where State Street intersects with Main, and where all our parades eventually show up. We have a lot of parades in Montpelier. In Tour #1 I described the epic Dewey Day parade in 1898, and our equally epic reenactment of it 100 years later. Our Independence Day parade and fireworks draws people from all over the state, which is why we always have it on July 3, so as to not pull all the Fourth of July cheer out of towns smaller than ours. On the first Sunday in May there's an All Species Day parade. It's an event with lots of colorful costumes, animals, puppets, music and pageantry, all meant to celebrate the diversity of life and the (entirely theoretical) arrival of spring.

Then, on the second Saturday in June we are one of about 70 cities that joins in the World Naked Bike Ride, which is exactly what it sounds like. An entirely different sort of ride happens on the second Saturday in August, when the United Motorcyclists of Vermont stage an annual Toy Run for Shriners Hospital. Several hundred motorcycles coast through the city carrying stuffed animals and other toys, and all are dropped off on the State House lawn. There was even once a circus parade in Montpelier.

In the late 1800s, PT Barnum's organization paraded its elaborate wagons and a herd of elephants through town. The much-anticipated star of that show was an enormous, whiskey-drinking elephant named Jumbo, and by all accounts at the time, he lived up to the hype.

At this intersection, State Street takes a little jog to the left and continues as East State Street all the way uphill to the Vermont College of Fine Arts that I talked about a few minutes ago. In earlier times, the East State Street hill was popular for sledding in the winter.

Up through the 1930s there were other streets the city would close off for sledding as well. Today, the most popular winter sliding hill is in our park located above the city.

Off the Beaten Path: Hubbard Park is another of those destinations that is so easily missed by visitors, but so worth a visit. It's a forested, 4-season park with lots of walking/skiing trails, picnic shelters and a stone observation tower that looks medieval but was built in 1915. The park is accessible from various points in the city. Anyone can give you driving directions if you need them, but if you'd like to get there with a fairly easy hike, the easiest route is a switchback trail behind the State House that leads directly up to Hubbard Park Tower.

Looking across at East State Street, on the right side you'll see an 1840s Federal style building. The space Blue Stone Pizza occupies has been a diner/restaurant under various owners and names since 1937, and its big front window is said to provide the best view in town. In the street next to it there once stood a five-story brick structure called the Arch Building, because of the drive-through arch placed in the middle of it. If you can't quite imagine a building sitting in the middle of a street, it's featured in an old photo you can see inside City Hall that shows this part of State Street in the mid-1800s.

A Bourbon in the Rubble

The complex on the opposite side of East State Street is called City Center and it's easy to tell it's the newest of all the downtown buildings.

The previous, late-19th century building on that corner had businesses ranging from dry goods to furniture and upholstery, undertaking services and a beloved clothing shop called The Children's Store that old-timers still mourn the loss of.

In the winter of 1980 that building, which now also housed an outlet of the state liquor store, was entirely gutted by fire in the middle of the night. I still remember that night myself.

I also remember my history-loving father venturing into the

rubble to retrieve a cultural artifact for posterity. That bottle of Ten High bourbon is still lurking somewhere inside my family home. And still unopened!

It Was Right There All the Time

Back on the corner of State and Main, looking across the street from the TD Bank building you'll see a red-painted Federal-style building which happens to be the oldest merchant building still standing in Montpelier. It escaped the great fire of 1875 largely because it was one of the only things made of brick on Main Street at that time. If we could return to the 1970s – not that we'd want to – we would not be looking at this gorgeously preserved example of early Federal-style architecture. Instead, we'd see an unremarkable structure covered in aluminum siding,

with walls of plate glass windows wrapped around the ground floor and surrounded by sheets of some dark, formica-style material. It was the site of another popular clothing store called the Vogue

Shop. Those of us who didn't know any better thought nothing of its appearance at the time, but in the 1980s it was gloriously restored to its original 1826 appearance. Looking now at the beautiful brick façade and ground-floor bay windows, it's hard to believe anyone ever had the nerve to cover it up.

EAT, DRINK AND SHOP

A few words about all the good things near this intersection: Over at the City Center, along with the **Artist's Hand** - a store showcasing the work of local artists – and the **Skinny Pancake**, which offers mouth-watering crepes, the City Center has a bakery called **La Brioche**. Here, you can get whatever delicious things the students of the New England Culinary Institute are whipping up that day. "NECI", as it is informally called, was founded in Montpelier in 1980, and its most famous alum is Alton Brown, the host of the Food Network's Iron Chef America and Good Eats. A little farther up Main Street, the Institute also run **NECI on Main**, a full-service restaurant with a downstairs pub that offers a great tapas menu.

I've already mentioned **Blue Stone**, where you'll get great pizza along with your fabulous view of the crossroads. Before leaving State Street, I'll just also also mention **Cool Jewels**, which has been anchoring the corner of Main and State for years, offering all sorts of beads, necklaces and crystals. **Katie's Jewels** next door offers fine jewelry and repairs, and next door to that is the cozy and comfortable **Ondine Salon**. And don't forget the **AroMed** aromatherapy shop which has a delicious assortment of essential oils and was one of the first businesses in the area to really begin exploring the uses of CBD oil.

STOP 2.8 - THE SECRET IN THE MIDDLE

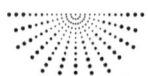

67-77 MAIN STREET, BLANCHARD BLOCK

We have one more historical block to talk about before ending this tour. It's directly across from the Cool Jewels store, and as the name on its top pediment suggests, it was the ambitious project of a man named Asa Blanchard. He owned a tannery in Vergennes before moving to Montpelier to become a real estate magnate. To make room for his building, he tore down the oldest place in Montpelier, the Cadwell House. Built around 1790, it had badly deteriorated, but in its heyday had been a fashionable rooming house and center of city life. There's a plaque on the corner of the Blanchard building next to Bear Pond Books noting that the Cadwell House once accommodated U.S. President James Monroe, as well as the Marquis de Lafayette, America's greatest French ally in the Revolutionary War.

The Blanchard building is similar to many such blocks that can still be found in historic districts of small cities around the country, but this one had a secret that most others did not. You get some hint of it from the stately arched main entrance with the wide windows above it. While much of the building was dedicated to merchant and office space, in the rear of the top floors of his building, Asa Blanchard created an opera house, and not a small one. It was an opera house big enough to seat 800 people. For 25 years it attracted some of the country's top performers because it was conveniently located on the route between Boston and Montreal for traveling theater troupes. Audience members arrived from all over the state by train, and specially scheduled trolley cars were engaged at the end of each performance to carry Barre residents home again. The novel attraction of moving pictures eventually wore down the demand for live theater. The opera house staged its last performance in 1910. Unfortunately there is practically no remaining evidence of it inside now.

For a while in the early 20th century, an elite local organization called the Apollo Club made its home in the Blanchard Block, with several well-appointed rooms housing a library and pool room.

The slightly different style of building you see at the end of the block was added later to serve as a hall for the Grand Army of the Republic, which was a fraternal organization for Union veterans of the American Civil War.

The upper floors of the block are now used entirely for office space and apartments, but there is still a wonderfully vintage atmosphere to many of the retail shops on the ground floor - from the creak in an old floorboard to the occasional flashes of handsome woodwork. In my thoroughly unbiased opinion, all of them deserve a visit.

Eat, Drink and Shop

Bear Pond Books is a heavenly place for book lovers and regularly hosts lively, well-attended author events. The **No. 9 Boutique** next to it is a two-fer: women's clothing and jewelry up front, and in the rear an assortment of antiques, home decor and collectibles. **Guitar Sam** has been a fixture in different locations in town for over 38 years, and it was one of the first musical instrument stores to begin selling online in 1998. You could spend hours browsing the natural bath and body products and chatting with the friendly folks in **Splash Naturals**, and anchoring the block at the end is **Capitol Stationers**, a family-owned stationery and gift store that opened in 1950 and is your go-to stop for an "Eat More Kale" t-shirt. It's Montpelier's version of "Life is Good" and became a meme before we ever knew what a meme was.

That brings us to the end of Tour #2 in this series. I know I'm leaving you in the middle of the street, so if you are intending to keep walking along Main Street toward the Winooski River, you might want to skip on to Tour #5, which starts at Charlie-O's World Famous across the street. It's a tour that starts at a bar and ends at another one. What's better than that, right?! Hope to see you there!

TOUR 3 - ELM STREET MINI LOOP

JAILS, BAKERS AND CIVIC DRAMA

STOP 3.1 - MAIL ORDER LOCKUPS

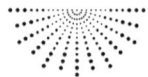

10 ELM STREET

*I*ntroduction
    Welcome to Tour #3 in the What Are You Looking At?! Walking Tours for Montpelier, VT. This time, we'll be starting from the Court House at the corner of Elm and State Streets. I've called this tour the mini-loop because a little farther up Elm Street it takes a right turn at School Street, another onto Main, and one more onto Langdon Street, which will bring you back to the Court House vicinity to complete the loop. The tour after this one is a larger loop that continues straight up Elm and connects with Main Street farther up. You don't have to remember all that, so don't worry. I'll give you the signal when we reach the spot where you can decide to either stay with the mini-loop or switch to the bigger loop and really stretch your legs.

Now, we'll get started by walking up Elm Street to our first stop, which is on the sidewalk near the fancy-looking brick building that shares a parking lot with the court house.

———

You might think this quaint-looking, Queen Anne-style building was designed to be the residence of some wealthy Montpelier family, but in fact it was purpose-built in 1900 as a jail house. It was an early example of a pre-fabricated kit, obtained by mail-order from the Pauly Jail Building Company, which is still going strong out in Noblesville, Illinois. This wasn't the first jail built on Elm Street. It was commissioned when the deterioration of the original jail reached such a state of decay that it was judged unfit for habitation, even by prisoners. At this time, the Pauly company was putting up state-of-the-art, steel-cage facilities all over the country and many of their turn-of-the-century designs have the same, rather grand and whimsically decorative architecture as this one. It gives the buildings a more welcoming aspect than anyone would really expect to find in a jail, but its residential appearance might also be because in those days the jailer and his family usually lived on site.

BIRTHPLACE OF OUR FARMERS MARKET

The jail closed in the early 70s and eventually the county sheriff's department moved in. The parking lot here was also the first home of our Farmers Market. The markets really started taking off throughout the country during the early 1990s, but ours has been in operation since 1977. As I mentioned earlier, it's now found on State Street in the lot next to Christ Church every Saturday from late spring until fall.

Let's go a few steps further up the street, where we'll get a look at the site of the city's original jail, and I will tell you the riveting story of a honeymoon that ended in murder.

STOP 3.2 - FOUNDERS AND ODDFELLOWS

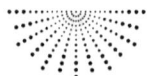

24 ELM STREET, JAILHOUSE COMMON

This area around Jailhouse Common is the site of Montpelier's first settlement – a modest log cabin built in 1787 where Jacob and Rebecca Davis and their sons first lived. They built a more substantial home the following year, and many years later Jacob's son Thomas gave that house to the city of Montpelier to serve as its first jail. A good deal of stone was brought in to create a sort of makeshift dungeon inside, but it wasn't long before something bigger was needed. A granite building went up first, and then finally a two-story version of the brick and granite building you see today.

Two Buildings in One

When it was abandoned in favor of the adorable Queen Anne jail next door, this building languished for several years until a big renovation got underway.

If you look at the wall where the front door is, you can see the difference in brickwork marking the outline of the original building before it was made wider and also taller by two stories. The gabled roof was also replaced with a flat one. All these changes were carried out by the new owners: the Independent Order of Odd Fellows. If you look up at the wall facing the street, you can still see their granite plaque in the middle, just below the roofline. If you have no idea who the Odd Fellows are I won't judge, because neither did I until I Googled them. It's a fraternal organization similar to Freemasons and others like them, with the secret handshakes and symbols and the auxiliary units with names that sound vaguely dystopian. They are still in existence today and do a lot of charitable work, but their real heyday was in the late 19th and early 20th centuries.

Oddfellows building - looking towards State, with old courthouse in background, and Chirst Church with original steeple

Off the Beaten Path: The building is filled with offices now, but you can follow the shaded path to a hidden spot around the back that leads to **The Cheshire Cat**. It is a fun and funky store filled with unique and beautiful jewelry, hand-designed clothing and other fun stuff. I want to strongly recommend you make your way back there, not only for the store, but because you will find a wonderfully quiet, leafy corner with benches, where you can sit while I tell you the story of Laura Cutler-Gould-Caswell and her two husbands, one of whom ended up imprisoned in this very jail.

STOP 3.3 - THE OLD (LOVE) TRIANGLE

JAILHOUSE COMMON POCKET PARK

*L*aura Cutler was born in 1851 on a farm in East Montpelier, which is a few miles outside of town. Whether she had other suitors in her early 20s is unknown, but we do know that sometime in the 1870s her father took on a hired hand named James Sherman Caswell, and "Sherm", as he was called, fell in love with her. With his heart set on marrying Laura he started wooing, and since he was a handsome Civil War veteran with a pension, Laura was not opposed.

Her father, Willard, was a different story. Sherm was known for wandering off into town to take a drink or two...or ten, and he was known for being a mean drunk, so although she was well into her 30s, on a farm in the middle of nowhere with no other particular prospects on the horizon, Willard Cutler – God love him – thought his daughter could do better, and he put his foot down. No marriage.

Then, Willard died. You might think we're heading for a happy ending now, right? Well, hold on. While her father's estate was getting sorted out, Laura took on extra help to run the farm. Another hired hand named George Gould arrived on the scene, and by the end of the summer she'd decided to marry him instead. Poor Sherm was kicked to the curb and asked to clear out while the newlyweds were on their honeymoon. He didn't, though. Instead, he got himself a bottle and sat drinking in his room, which did not improve his mood.

When the couple returned from the honeymoon, Sherm poked his head and a very big shotgun out from a second story window and shot George Gould dead. It was such a powerful charge of ammunition that the newspapers report it swiped the mustache right off George's face. Laura fled to a neighbor's while Sherm, immediately filled with remorse, turned himself in to a neighbor, who hitched up his horse and wagon and calmly drove him in to Montpelier for booking.

The trial was quite a spectacle, but the real show-stopper came after it was over. On the same day that Sherman Caswell received his life sentence, he got married. To Laura. Throughout the trial, the widow of the man he'd murdered visited him faithfully in jail, and held his hand through the bars of the cell while the vows were recited. A few years later, apparently feeling there wasn't much future in the relationship, Laura sued for divorce. She remained on her farm for the rest of her life, while Sherm was eventually pardoned through the efforts of a group of Civil War veterans. He spent his remaining days in the Union House Hotel in Montpelier.

The Birth of a Broadway Hit

That does it for jail talk. We'll do some walking and talking now as we continue up Elm Street, but before we start have a look across the street at Sweet Melissa's. It was built in the 1850s by James Langdon, who I mentioned in the last tour, and it's another of the city's moveable houses. When first constructed it sat at the other end of Langdon Street on the corner of Main. It was also the city's police station at one time. The police are all gone now, and Sweet Melissa's is not only a very friendly bar it's also a fantastic, intimate venue for live music of every genre. If you go, you might be one of the first to witness a future Broadway sensation, because this is where Montpelier native

Anais Mitchell, the creator of the Tony award-winning musical "Hadestown" got started.

Eat, Drink and Shop

Walking on we see **Grian Herbs** on the left, which is named for a Celtic sun goddess. A visit to the apothecary inside is like taking a little wander back in time. It's also a feast for the senses, with its selection of tinctures, syrups, elixirs, salves and whatever else you can do with an herb, and they also have a selection of clothing, jewelry and crafts.

As we continue on, we're passing a few more restaurants as well. **The Royal Orchid** has all your well-known Thai favorites and has been in town for years, and across the street is the **Hippie Chickpea**, which we've been delighted to welcome as Montpelier's first restaurant dedicated to Middle Eastern cuisine. The homemade pita and baklava is not to be missed. When we reach the intersection up ahead, you can also check out the **Uncommon Market and Deli**. They've got a wonderful open-air seating area on a side porch that overlooks the river, and they specialize in a full range of super-fresh seafood.

Welcome to the Jungle Room

The building now occupied by Hippie Chickpea had a bar in it for many years starting in the 1950s, but then in the early 80s, a new business moved in that had the townsfolk intrigued. It was called the Blue Heron Hot Tub Spa. They seem ubiquitous now, but in the 80s hot tubs were a fascinating novelty and these spas were popping up all over, renting "tub time" to their customers.

The Blue Heron had a "bathing suits optional" policy and theme-based environments with names like "The Jungle Room". It quickly earned a racy reputation and was the talk of the town for a while. It all went bust before long, though. It might have been hygiene issues – the early days of hot tubs were known for that – but there were also rumors of unsanctioned videotaping. Whatever the reason, the owners slipped away under cover of darkness one night and were never seen again, and that was the end of the "tub-timing" in Montpelier.

STOP 3.4 - AN UNCOMMON VIEW

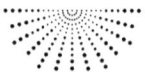

CORNER OF ELM & STATE STREETS

*H*ere, where Elm and School Streets intersect, the Uncommon Market is in a brick building that's had a corner store in it for as long as anyone can remember, and that's going back to the 1800s. On the diagonal corner is a house set on a slope with several flights of stone steps leading to its front door. It doesn't look as old as it is, but it was built in the early 1800s and the entire area that encompasses the corner house and the Victorian next to it was once a single estate that had a croquet court on the lower part of the lawn.

Off the Beaten Path: If you are game for a short but steep hike, next to that Victorian house is Hillside Avenue, which leads to Cliff Street, which will take you to one of the most-photographed views of Montpelier. You may have seen it featured in some website story about us. It seems to have become the go-to photo for any story about the city, but that's really only been in the last few years. I know the first time many of us saw this view, it was in a photo featuring a gorgeously twilit scene filled with church steeples in a town surrounded by forested hills, and we said "Oh, how beautiful! Where is it?"

Hillside Avenue and Cliff Streets are not extremely busy, but you do need to take care on the hike because there are no sidewalks. If you were to continue past the viewpoint, you'd come to a sign directing you to another of the many entrances to Hubbard Park.

Extended Loop Walkers Exit Here!

Back down here at this four-way intersection, we have also reached the point where you can continue the mini-loop tour or switch to Tour #4, which continues straight up Elm Street and connects to Main Street farther up. The list of stops for Tour #4 will tell you what's in store along that route.

An Early Champion for Education

For those of us staying on the mini-loop, we'll turn right here and cross the bridge over the North Branch of the Winooski River. In the early 1990s, this bridge became the first structure in the city to be named after a woman. The VT Legislature renamed it the Rose Lucia Bridge. It honored the Vermont teacher, principal and supervisor of local schools who lived most of her life in Montpelier.

She was passionate about improving the quality of education in rural schools and was an early adopter of the Montessori method. She was also the author of the "Peter and Polly" series of children's books. Written between 1912-1915, they told the story of two siblings growing up in St. Johnsbury, VT. They were distributed internationally, and recently the Kellogg-Hubbard Library published a combined edition of the series and they have copies available for purchase.

Our next stop will be at the corner of School and Main Streets, in front of the Unitarian Church.

STOP 3.5 - THE INTERSECTION OF FAITH

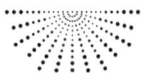

130 MAIN STREET, UNITARIAN CHURCH

This church is on the site of the first tavern and inn in Montpelier, operated in the 1790s by none other than the ubiquitous Davis family. It became known as the Union House, and several versions of this accommodation literally went up in flames over the years. The last version was across the street where the bank is now, where Sherm Caswell spent his last years, and that eventually burned also.

CHURCH AND STATE?!

When the Unitarian Universalists first formed a congregation in Montpelier, they had an arrangement that will probably never be repeated in the modern era. They held their meetings at the State House. This didn't really suit anyone, though, so a committee of businessmen in the congregation commissioned Boston architect Thomas Silloway to design this church in 1865. It was originally painted a light gray. At some point it was painted all over wedding-cake-white, which oddly enough seemed to make it almost invisible. More recently it was repainted in this sage color with white accents and when it was finished it was like it had suddenly stepped from behind a curtain and we were all stunned to realize how beautiful it was.

The Itinerant Organ Maker

If the church is open you should have a peek inside for a better look at the hand-painted windows, the dark walnut pews, and their gloriously restored 1866 pipe organ, built by George Stevens of Cambridge, MA, who was a sort of Johnny Appleseed of organs.

He is said to have installed about 800 of them in churches around the country. This church is also the venue of choice for many classical music concerts. If you are a fan of chamber music, check to see if anything is on during your visit, because for a fraction of what you'd pay in larger cities, you will get to hear world-class musicians in an amazing setting.

Our Scenic Spires

At this intersection, we have in our sights all four of the church spires that are a major feature of the scenic hilltop view I spoke about earlier. As you face the library, to the left is the Trinity Methodist. You may want to capture a photo of its steeple, colorfully decorated with hearts and chevrons. If you are lucky enough to be here on the first Saturday in October, don't miss the chance to experience one of the two seatings for their annual chicken pie supper. This is an annual October tradition for churches throughout Vermont. Don't call them "pot pies"! It's just "chicken pie" and it's cooked with biscuits on top rather than pie crust.

Further down School Street you can just get a peek at the First Baptist Church, built in the classic New England Gothic style in 1868, and on the corner opposite the library is the United Church of

Christ's Bethany Church. It was also originally built in 1868 but when it became unstable its red stone blocks were taken down, stone by stone, and then reincorporated into the more modern church that was completed in 1959. The interior includes a chapel with a labyrinth that is open to the public at scheduled times.

Let's cross the street now for our next stop at the library. Its origin is a story of high drama, greed and redemption, with yet another little ghostly angle thrown on top. There are some benches on the lawn if you'd like to rest your feet while I tell you all about it.

STOP 3.6 - THE KELLOGG-HUBBARD HUBBUB

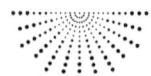

135 MAIN STREET

The saga of Montpelier's public library begins in the waning months of 1889 in a fashionable neighborhood of New York City, where Martin Kellogg, a Barre VT native who'd struck it rich in the real estate market, suddenly dropped dead of a heart attack. Less than three months later his wife, Montpelier native Fanny Hubbard Kellogg, followed him, and Montpelier soon learned their entire estate had been bequeathed to the city for two projects – the construction of a chapel and gates at Green Mount Cemetery, and the building of a public library in the center of town.

HUBBARD HAS HIS DAY IN COURT

Any celebration was short-lived, though. Fanny's nephew, John Hubbard, knew a thing or two about real estate himself. In the mid-1800s his family owned more real estate than anyone in Montpelier, including a substantial area of town known as Hubbard's Meadow, which the family had laid out in streets and developed. You can visit that neighborhood on Tour #4.

John had been hoping for something quite a bit different from his aunt's will, and he was a sore loser. When it was brought up for a ruling in probate court, the two witnesses to the will were present. They were learned men, not just some strangers who'd been pulled from the street and presented with a pen. One witness was Fanny's physician and the other a law clerk, but once in court Fanny Kellogg's attorney listened, no doubt with his jaw hanging open, as the two men suddenly sounded very unclear on the concept. *"Will? That was a will? I had no idea that was a will."*

The will was declared invalid.

No Peace in the Village

The city erupted in outrage, cried foul and filed a suit, but just before the ruling was expected, the town selectmen suddenly calmed down and agreed to a compromise. They withdrew their claim in exchange for Hubbard's promise to grant Montpelier a very modest sum to build the library.

There were enough suspicions over all this to rip the city apart. As construction of the new library continued, an effort was mounted to fund a rival library, hoping to ensure the Hubbard-funded library's failure. The revered local artist Thomas Waterman Wood was recruited to the cause. He agreed to give 42 oil paintings to establish a gallery in the rival library.

Even after both libraries opened in 1896, the conflict continued. There were heated town meetings where Hubbard factions and anti-Hubbard factions hurled abuse at each other. Then, a most extraordinary thing happened.

Hubbard Has the Last Word

In 1899, John Hubbard died, ostensibly of liver cancer, but perhaps also from the strain of living as the town pariah. When his will became public, the people of Montpelier learned it had been dated two years before his death, and that Hubbard had left the bulk of his estate to the city. Not only was there a sizable bequest for the library and cemetery, he had also gifted the city 100 acres of the land known as Hubbard Hill, along with enough money to turn it into a city park.

Presumably, there were a lot of sheepish faces around town at the time, and the Montpelier *Evening Argus* reported what many must have been thinking: "Even those who have said very hard things about him previously are softened today, and some have acknowledged that they might possibly have judged him too harshly."

With that, Montpelier's love affair with its public library took root and has never faltered since. As to the building itself, the exterior is made of rusticated granite blocks quarried in Dummerston. The columns in the first and second story porticos are pink granite from North Conway, NH. The inside is gorgeously restored with oak staircases, marble fireplaces and an overhead central skylight, and there is a collection of marble friezes on the second floor, which ironically at one time housed the Thomas Waterman Wood collection!

Another large bequest in the 1990s made it possible to add a large wing to the back of the building. With the added capacity, there is ALWAYS something going on – language club meetings, spelling bees, lectures, book sales, author talks, you name it. If you walk by on an early winter evening, you'll see all the lights are on, and the golden glow pouring out its many windows make it look like a lantern in the darkness.

It's well worth a visit, and don't forget to snap a selfie with the library mouse near the front door.

And here is the ghostly codicil I promised. At Green Mount Cemetery at the lower end of State Street, high up on its hillside you'll find John Hubbard's gravesite and the expansive memorial dedicated to his memory. There is a bronze sculpture of a seated male figure, weathered with verdigris. Its official name is *Thanatopsis*, a Greek word meaning "a consideration of death", but the  sculpture's more popular name is Black Agnes. The folk tale is that the statue carries a curse, so that anyone who sits in the figure's lap when the moon is full at midnight, will be haunted by misfortune and an early death. You can find out more from a book called *Montpelier Chronicles* by local historian Paul Heller, and yes, they do have a copy of it in the library.

Before we continue down Main Street, I'll invite you to make a quick side trip with me to the house on School Street that's right next to the library. I make it a point to visit this house often, and if you follow me, you'll see why.

STOP 3.7 - A BAKER'S DOZEN...OF LAWYERS?!

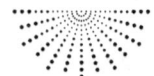

28 SCHOOL STREET

Okay, so there's a sign out front that gives it away. We have arrived at the home of Manghi's Bread, which opened in Montpelier in 1981. With the explosion of the local food movement over the past 10 years, we are spoiled for choice in Central Vermont when it comes to homestyle breads, but before any of that got rolling there were the Manghis. Elaine and Paul started the business in their home in North Randolph in the 1970s before moving the operation to Montpelier, and the bakery is now under the direction of their daughter Maria. Inside, you are immediately in the midst of a real, working bakery and enveloped in the sights and fragrance of fresh-baked loaves. There's no café or fancy display case, and everything is so informal that you may think they aren't set up to serve retail customers but they most certainly are. You may very well walk away holding something still warm from the oven. They are open from 7am-5pm Monday through Friday.

SUCH A CLAN OF ATTORNEYS!

The house they are in is one of the oldest in Montpelier, built in the early 1800s by Samuel Prentiss, who lived there with his wife

Lucretia, who gave birth to no less than 12 children. Two died in infancy, but the rest, all boys, grew up in the house, and all ten of them studied law, following in their father's footsteps. As an earlier guide for the city remarked, "Montpelier will probably never again bring forth such a clan of attorneys!"

The Forebears of Your Guide :)

Before leaving this area, I can't resist giving a shout-out to the large white house next door

and my own family's roots. Established in 1921, the Guare & Sons Funeral Home is the oldest family-owned business in Montpelier that is still in operation.

It was established by my grandparents, Thomas J. Guare and Florence Emmons Guare, and although I can't prove it, my grandmother was almost certainly the first female licensed embalmer in the area.

We'll head back now and cross Main Street to reach our next stop somewhere near where Yankee Wine & Spirits meets the Main Street Grill. Before crossing, pause at the corner as this is the best vantage point for viewing the large "Restaurant" sign on top of the building next to the liquor store. This is a historic neon sign and it is fitting that it still blazes bright over a site that has housed a restaurant since at least the 1870s. Once we cross the street I will tell you how ironic it is that the Vermont State Liquor Store ended up on this corner.

STOP 3.8 - FROM NEAR BEER TO CRAFT BEER

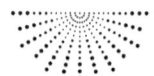

118 MAIN STREET

As I mentioned earlier, the New England Culinary Institute came to Montpelier in 1980. This restaurant, NECI on Main, is more commonly known by locals as the Main Street Grill, and like the La Brioche bakery down the street, it's another spot where you can get a bird's-eye view of the culinary students learning their craft while they whisk their sauces and braise their meats. It's got a full-service dining room on the main floor, and a pub below that specializes in creative tapas menus. At one time, they had a third option for upscale dining at the Chef's Table, but that is now a private function space.

In the 1960s and 70s, this was the Lobster Pot, which had a bar on one side and a restaurant on the other. The neon sign that spanned the two doorways was nearly as big as the one on the roof, and had the added feature of a neon-lit lobster. The restaurant had the area's first salad bar – a true "salad boat" in keeping with the nautical interior, and it was THE place for dining out in Montpelier for a couple of decades.

Now You See Them, Now You Don't

Earlier still, this was the site of Miller's Inn, which got rolling in the 1880s, in the middle of Vermont's Prohibition era. William Miller was the proprietor, and the inn was an expansion of his grocery and bottling business. He bottled a number of different beverages – ginger ale, cider, club soda – but his most popular item was a near-beer called "Uno". It operated on something of a legal razor's edge. A lengthy court case had not been able to determine if it violated the liquor laws or not. He was raided in 1892 but nothing illegal was found. There's an old folk tale that Miller kept his "special stock" on a hinged shelf above a covered hole in the floor. A flick of his wrist and all evidence disappeared at the first sign of trouble.

It's interesting to note that while federal prohibition ran for 13 years between 1920 and 1933, Vermont's law was enacted in 1852, so we were dry for over 80 years! It's hard to believe we lasted that long, but we seem to be making up for lost time. If you are looking for some of the famous Vermont-made craft brews and distilled spirits, you will find a wide assortment in **Yankee Wines and Spirits**. On shelves that need no hinges.

Eat, Drink and Shop

If you can't wait to try a sample of what the Hill Farmstead brewers are offering, just walk half a block farther down the street and pull up a stool at the **Three Penny Taproom**. It has an ever-changing handwritten tap list of 24 options on draft, along with a full line of locally distilled liquors as well as all the usual brands from near and far. It's also got a pretty lip-smacking food menu, which you can enjoy at the bar or in their dining room. Food is available 11-9 weekdays, Noon-10 Saturdays and Noon-4 on Sundays.

Right next door to Three Penny is **Down Home Kitchen**, which is

Montpelier's homage to Southern-style cooking. It is open every day from 8am until 2pm. Fried chicken, catfish, fluffy biscuits, cheese grits, and a lot more. Everything is delicious but their specialty is breakfast. Along with traditional restaurant seating they have one long common table running down the middle of the room. Grab a seat there if you are feeling social and interested in meeting new people.

If you've been walking while I talk, you should be at the corner of Main and Langdon Streets now. This will be our final stop, where I will share the secret of one of Montpelier's earliest – and biggest – homegrown industries.

STOP 3.9 - IT AIN'T THE RITZ

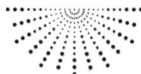

CORNER OF MAIN & LANGDON STREETS

*I*f I say the words "cracker barrel", it might make you think of that family-friendly restaurant chain that has an outpost off highway exits all over America. But at one time the meaning was a literal one. There were actual barrels filled with actual crackers, and like the pot-belly stove, they served as a gathering point for chatter and gossip at local country stores in days of yore. These barrels were not filled with crackers of the Ritz, saltine, oyster or Keebler variety. They were shaped more like a biscuit, hard and round and about an inch thick, and they could be stored for months, if not years. They were known as "common crackers", and from 1828 until 1959 most of them were baked right across the street about where the AT&T store is now.

A Horse-Drawn Oven

It was known as Cross & Sons Baking Company. It was originally started by Timothy Cross, but his brother Charles took the business to a new level. In the early days he baked three days a week and delivered on the other two. He had a horse that worked the same schedule. Three days a week it pulled a revolving stone oven that baked the crackers, and two days a week it was hitched to the wagon for the deliveries. As time went on Cross was joined in the business by his sons and continued the partnership with his brother Timothy. Gradually they added more rooms, more ovens, and then finally a cracker-making machine that turned out to be a game-changer. By the end of the 1890s they were reportedly turning out 50,000 crackers a day.

After Charles died at the age of 93, his son Bart carried on for a few years, but then sold the business to George L. Edson, whose family is directly descended from – guess who? Our old friend and founding father, Jacob Davis. George, and later his son Lansdale, continued the business under the name of Cross & Sons, and for decades they made "Montpelier Crackers" a household name throughout New England. The company was also known as a progressive employer, one of the first in the country to offer insurance and a retirement system for its employees. The years after the second world war were not as kind, however. The Montpelier factory closed and operations moved to Claremont, NH, and by 1966 the company closed for good. But that wasn't the end of common crackers. They sold the recipe and all their machinery to Vrest Orton, the famous founder of the Vermont Country Store in Weston, Vermont. So, the Vermont Common Crackers you can buy today are essentially the same as the Montpelier Crackers that originated right here, over 190 years ago.

What do they taste like, you might ask? Well, they are not known as having a robust flavor on their own, but they have a way of making everything you eat with them better. If you toast them with some melted butter and Vermont cheddar, you might never eat a Ritz cracker again.

JAMES LANGDON'S SHOPPING MALL

We've come just about full circle now, and if you turn down Langdon Street to head back to our starting point at the Court House, you'll be strolling along one of Montpelier's early urban redevelopment projects. In the late 1800s, James Langdon had a vision for a fashionable shopping district in this area, and he's responsible for the building directly across from Down Home Kitchen. It's a handsome piece of architecture that fills the block between State Street and Langdon, and you'll notice the decorative granite blocks running up the building at each corner. These are called "quoins" and you can see the style repeated in the other buildings on Langdon Street.

EAT, DRINK AND SHOP

James Langdon didn't live long enough to see his shopping plaza dreams fulfilled, but today Langdon Street is a pleasant street with an array of eclectic shops. **Buch Spieler** is vinyl heaven for audiophiles and has been around for 45 years. Literally translated, the name means "book player". The original owners were two friends who took high school German together and it's not entirely clear whether they knew what they were doing when they landed on that name. Further down on the left you'll find **Global Gifts** with treasures small and large from around the world, and also **J Langdon**, which is a beautifully curated antiques shop.

On the right is **Onion River Outdoors**, which has a full inventory of sporting goods of all kinds for every season, and it also rents bikes, snowshoes, skis and ice skates. A little farther down is **Roam**, which has all the footwear and apparel you'll need to look good on the slopes or the hiking path. And finally, you've got another restaurant tucked away down here right in the middle of the street. The **Langdon Street Tavern** offers a variety of juicy burgers, chicken wings and other traditional tavern fare that you can enjoy in a booth, or you can sit at the bar and watch whatever sport is happening on the screens above.

And that's it for the mini-loop tour! If you continue across the Langdon Street bridge, you'll find yourself back where we started, or you can do a little more exploring along Main Street. If you decide to skip the bigger loop of Tour #4, you can catch up with me in front of Charlie-O's on Main Street for Tour #5. See you there!

TOUR 4 - ELM STREET EXTENDED LOOP

STATELY HOMES AND CAPTAINS OF INDUSTRY

STOP 4.1 - ELM STREET CEMETERY

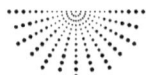

207 ELM STREET

Introduction
Hello, and welcome back! This is Tour #4, which begins at the corner of Elm and School Streets. The complete loop from this point is about a mile in length. The stops are widely spread out on this one, so it's a great option if you'd like to take an extended walk – or even a bike ride - without as much description. It ends at the Unitarian Church on Main Street, where Tour #3 picks up. I will let you know toward the end when we are rejoining the area that's covered in that tour, so you won't miss anything.

From this point we are going to start walking up Elm Street. You can choose either side of it, but our first stop will be a few blocks up at the city's oldest cemetery, which is on the right-hand side of the street.

About a half-block up from the intersection with School Street, have a look at the large cliff on the left-hand side. At the top is the lookout point for the city view I mentioned in the last tour, and that viewing spot was largely made possible by an event that took place here in

2005. It was a snowy Monday evening on the day after Christmas when one of the neighborhood's residents heard what he thought was the snowplow going by.

Except the plow kept getting louder, and closer. Turns out it was a massive rockslide. Full-sized trees and 30-ton boulders as big as cars came hurtling 60 feet down to spread across the street. It took out power lines and everything else in its path. Miraculously, it all came to a rumbling stop at the doorstep of the apartment building across the street, and no one was injured. Another miracle was that the slide did not extend to any of the homes that are rather precariously perched on the edge of Cliff Street above, which you can see if you peer up through the greenery to the left of the lookout point.

A Grid-Shaped Meadow

Walking further up the street, at the intersection of Elm and Spring we're entering an area once known as Hubbard Meadow. On a map you can see it's the only neighborhood in town with a neatly laid out grid pattern, and that's because it was an early housing development mapped out by the Hubbard family in the early 1800s. I have more to say about one of the members of that family in tour #3 when we talk about the public library. Spring Street, as well as Winter Street next to it, both lead to an access road into Hubbard Park, and it's the only route in that allows vehicular traffic.

Our Founding Father's Resting Place

This cemetery dates back to 1813 and is the oldest in the city. It was originally leased to the town by the honorable Jeduthun Loomis, an early upstanding citizen and Judge who agreed not to pasture cows and horses on the land but reserved the right to have a few calves and sheep roaming around. He is not buried here, but Montpelier's founding father is. The grave of Colonel Jacob Davis is close to the street and fairly easy to pinpoint because of the American flags and the Revolutionary War medallion next to his tombstone. The engraving on the stone is faint, but he died in 1814 at the age of 72. His wife Rebecca lies next to him. An early history of Montpelier reports "…she was the never failing friend of the needy and distressed, the judicious adviser of the young, and the universal object of the love and respect of all classes of the people of the settlement."

A lot of the slate tombstones are too worn to read, but the cemetery is well maintained and if you visit at the right time you'll see a gorgeous line of blooming hydrangea bushes bordering the street.

When you're finished at the cemetery, continue up Elm Street and about a block past Winter Street you'll see a white, colonnaded house on the left-hand side of the street, which is our next stop.

STOP 4.2 - OUR BIG, FAT, GREEK LOVE AFFAIR

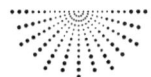

242 ELM STREET

*A*part from the State House and Court House, we haven't seen too many examples of this type of Greek Revival architecture on our tours, but here is one, and you'll see a few more like it on this tour. They conjure a southern antebellum state of mind that makes you think Scarlet O'Hara might slip out the door and glide down the portico. Like most of the country, Montpelier had a mid-19th century love affair with this style, which is characterized by the colonnaded portico and pedimented gable. They are known for having a symmetrical layout, but a particularly New England variation of this style places the front door off to the side as it is here. This house dates back to around 1850 and is thought to have been constructed by Alfred Wainwright, who owned the forerunner to Montpelier's historic Lane Manufacturing Company, which we'll hear more about in a few minutes.

We're going to keep going up Elm Street a bit farther and eventually turn right onto Vine Street, but before we do I invite you to pass by that intersection and walk on to Birchgrove Bakery.

STOP 4.3 - A BUTCHER, THEN A BAKER

279 ELM STREET

We are honestly unrivaled when it comes to top shelf bakeries in Montpelier, and this is another that should be on your pastry pilgrimage through the city. The shoebox-shaped building doesn't look particularly historic but it dates back to at least the 1950s when it operated as Joe's Market. As Montpelier continued to grow during the 20th century, an assortment of small, family-owned groceries set up shop in its expanding neighborhoods and residents were very loyal to their hyper-local markets and their very own meat butcher. Here in the Meadow, families shopped at the Meadow Mart, which is still in operation across the street, but they got their meat from Joe Canales here in this building, and other provisions as well.

An earlier bakery briefly operated here, and on opening day the baker had her sister pitching in to hand out the macaroons. That was kind of exciting for us because her sister is a movie star: Sandra Bullock. The Bullocks moved on quickly, though. The current owners Jennifer and John have decades of professional culinary experience between them, and Birchgrove Baking has it all – breakfast pastries, tarts, cookies and cheesecakes. They particularly specialize in customized cakes, such as the incomparable lemon meringue cake. It opens at 7 am on weekdays and 8am Saturday and Sunday. The closing times vary but it is always open until at least 2pm. I will be good and wait here on the sidewalk while you indulge.

STOP 4.4 - ATTRACTIONS FARTHER AFIELD

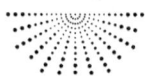

A REVIEW OF UPPER ELM STREET

*H*ere's a few final words on what you'll find if you come back later and continue on up Elm Street.

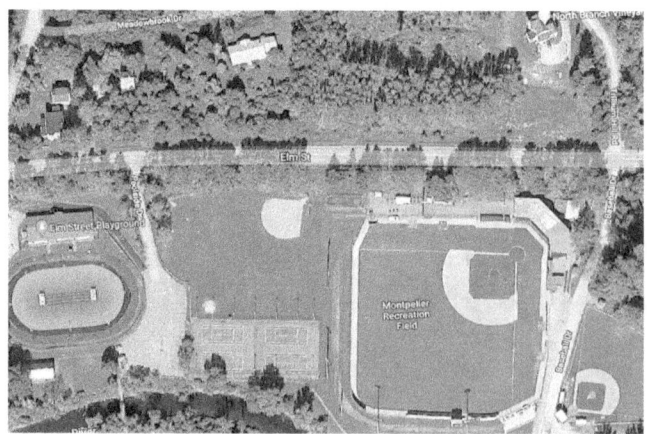

First, our spacious, oval-shaped municipal swimming pool is about a mile further up the road. Right next to the pool is the Recreation Field where on evenings in June and July you can grab a seat in the grandstand and cheer on the Vermont Mountaineers, our hometown team in the New England Collegiate Baseball League.

Right across the street from the field's entrance is a road that leads to North Branch Vineyards. They having tasting room hours on the weekends except for the period between January and March.

Farther down the road you'll find the North Branch Nature Center with a network of trails that wind through forest and field areas on a bend of the Winooski River. They offer all kinds of programs and special events for both children and adults, and you can access the river for swimming.

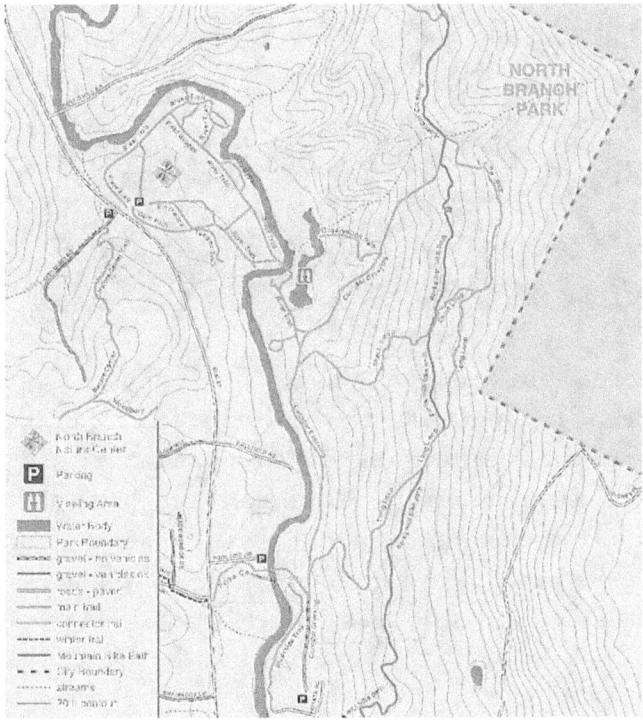

Finally, if you are looking for a wider expanse of water, keep driving (or pedaling) for another few miles to reach Wrightsville Beach, where you'll find a sandy beach, picnic sites with grills, rentals for canoes, kayaks and paddle boats, and an 18-hole disc golf course. The park has been kept in a very natural state – there are no fancy amenities, not even a snack stand. It is a little bit of heaven just a five-minute drive from the center of town, and if you are here during a heat wave, the temperature will be 5-10 degrees cooler out there.

Now, we'll retrace our steps to the intersection of Elm and Vine streets. Before turning left to cross the bridge, take a quick peek at the house across the street with the fire escape stairs over the porch. At one time it was more ornate, with decoratively patterned roof tiles and iron filigree along the roofline. It was the home of an inventor named Dennis Lane, and we are going to hear more about a particular invention of his that transformed this neighborhood in the late 1800s.

STOP 4.5 - WHAT IS A SAWMILL, ANYWAY?!

VINE STREET BRIDGE

I think of this part of town as one of Montpelier's hidden gems. This pedestrian bridge crosses over a picturesque section of the North Branch called Waterman Falls, and it leads to a leafy green and shaded neighborhood that we are going to walk through next. This is the area where that Greek Revival homeowner Alfred Wainwright started his iron foundry, but before that, in the earliest days of Montpelier the ubiquitous Jacob Davis sited a mill near the waterfall.

Now, I don't know about you, but whenever I thought of the term "sawmill" I always envisioned an old barn board building with a waterwheel next to a river. That's not exactly wrong, but a sawmill is more accurately described as the actual machinery that's inside it and used to…well, saw the wood. Tinkering with sawmill machinery was the particular genius of Dennis Lane, and I'll tell you a bit about why that was so important. Cross over the bridge and turn right to begin strolling through the Lane Shops neighborhood.

STOP 4.6 - THE BIRTH OF 2X4 LUMBER

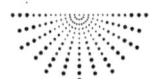

3 MECHANIC STREET

*D*ennis Lane started out as a sawmill operator in Barre, but he was also an inventor, and a tinkerer. He kept adjusting and tweaking the machinery until he finally came up with a new technology he patented as the Lever Cut Circular Saw Mill. With that, he got out of the business of operating a sawmill and into the business of manufacturing them.

Dennis went into business with Colonel Perley Pitkin, who you might remember from Tour #2 as the fire chief and principal hero in the battle to contain Montpelier's 1875 fire. These two were later joined by local attorney John Brock, and they formed the Lane Manufacturing  Company to build state-of-the-art sawmill machinery. They purchased the long brick building you see arranged to the right along the riverside, which had been the iron forge operated by Alfred Wainwright. Their headquarters office was on the site of this building on the left with the surrounding covered porch. The community building that's here now was completed in 1980, but was constructed to imitate the features of the 1870 original.

THE MANUFACTURING PLANT OF THE LANE MANUFACTURING COMPANY, MONTPELIER, VT., U. S. A.

The business was a roaring success. The patented Lane technology was the first to provide lumber of a consistent thickness. It featured a mechanical method for propelling the log through the blade, and it quickly became the nationwide, and then global, standard. It might be fair to say that the two-by-fours found in every wood-framed house in the world were first made possible by Dennis Lane.

Tragically, Lane died in 1888, just as the company was reaching the height of its success. He never knew that one of his circular sawmills was shipped four thousand miles up the Amazon River in Peru, or that others made their way to every corner of globe, from Chile to Sweden to Alaska and all points in between. Under the stewardship of his partners the business continued on and was picked up by a second generation, but with the Great Depression it fell on hard times and never really recovered. The company closed in 1961 and the building remained deserted and increasingly derelict for many years.

A Glorious Renaissance

During a brief spell in the 1970s the second floor of the building across from the community building served as a dance club called

Blackie Stone's Industrial Revolution, and it was about as sketchy as it sounds. Also, in the 1970s, Dennis Lane's great grandson reopened part of the plant to manufacture replacement parts for the sawmills, some of which are still in operation to this day. That business succumbed to fire in the late 70s, and shortly after that the entire complex underwent a glorious renaissance when it was developed into the residential area you see now.

The riverside condominiums are in the original main machine shop of Lane Manufacturing. This is such a charming and obviously desirable neighborhood that you might think it's a spot meant for people with lots of disposable income, but in fact it is managed by the Montpelier Housing Authority, with apartments rented to senior citizens at subsidized rates.

The Old Hubbard Home

At its apex, the Lane company had over 500 employees. It also comprised about 15 buildings in the Mechanic and Franklin Street area, so the atmosphere of the neighborhood was much more industrial at one time. It's hard to imagine the belching smokestacks and clanging machinery now as you stroll down Franklin Street. As you continue heading toward Main Street, you'll come to another rather magnificent looking Greek Revival, including the full treatment of Doric columned portico and a filigreed iron railing on two stories. This was the home of Roger Hubbard and his bachelor son John, who we hear more of in Tour #3. They didn't live on Franklin Street, though. This house once sat on Main Street on a spot that we'll pass in a few more minutes.

Past the Hubbard house you'll come to Main Street Middle School as you near the end of Franklin. This started out in 1914 as the city's first public high school. It was replaced by the current high school, which was built in 1956 at the edge of town near the interstate, although the interstate didn't exist at that time.

Once you reach Main Street, we'll be turning right to make our way back to the center of town, but if you just can't get enough of our architectural treasures, you can make a quick detour about a hundred feet up to the school's parking lot to look across the street at a building that represents one of our finest examples of the French Second Empire style, built around 1880.

If you walk past to look at it from the side, it might remind you just a little bit of the Addams Family house. Moving back down Main Street, you'll pass the intersection with Liberty Street, which I noted as an Off the Beaten Path recommendation in Tour #1. The Liberty/Loomis Street neighborhood offers more views of handsome and festively painted old homes.

STOP 4.7 - AROUND WE GO

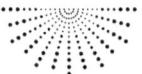

156 MAIN STREET ROUNDABOUT

So now we're here at Keck Circle, installed in the year 1995. It is not just Montpelier's first roundabout, but the first modern roundabout on a state road in the entire country! How about us, huh?! At first the traffic got backed up because we weren't quite sure how a roundabout worked, so we acted like it was just a really big and circular 4-way intersection, but we eventually got the hang of it.

On the north side of the circle is the Montpelier Health Center, which was originally built as a Masonic Temple. Before its construction, the house standing here was that Greek Revival of Roger Hubbard's that we just saw on Franklin Street. We are going to cross at the crosswalk in front of the bridge and make our way past the candy-colored house on the other side, another example of the festive Queen Anne-style "Painted Lady" architecture mentioned in our first tour. Across from it is an apartment building operated by the Montpelier Housing Authority. Next to that is the privately operated Gary Residence. It was built in the 1940s with a gift from the estate of Dr. Clara Gary, who was the first woman in Vermont to enter the medical profession. It started as a senior residence for women but now includes male residents also.

You can continue down Main Street on either side of the street as I'll be highlighting a few buildings on both sides. Our next stop will be in front of the Inn at Montpelier. If you happen to be staying there you may already know its history, but if not I'll give you the highlights.

STOP 4.8 - A CREDITOR, A SENATOR AND A CARPENTER WALK INTO A HOTEL...

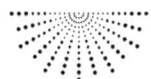

147-149 MAIN STREET - INN AT MONTPELIER

The Inn at Montpelier is spread between two buildings, one made of yellow-painted brick on the left, and a white-painted wooden one on the right. The Federal-style white house is the older of the two. Built around 1807, it's another of the few remaining wooden frame houses from the early days of Montpelier.

A Finger in Too Many Pies

The first owners were Chester Houghton and his wife, Hetty. Chester was a feverishly active merchant in town. He had a general store, a tavern, leased a distillery, was in the tin business, and then later invested heavily in a store, mill and potash operation in North-field. In short order he became overextended, and lost the house. His creditor briefly took possession before selling it to William Upham, a prominent lawyer who became a US Senator in 1842, one of only two Montpelier residents to hold the title. The other is the currently serving Patrick Leahy.

By the time Senator Upham died, his widow sold the house to the owner of the yellow brick home next door. This was none other than

James R. Langdon, who we've encountered a few times on these tours. At the time, the grand covered porch had not yet been added. It had been the home for many years of Dr. Edward Lamb, a revered physician lauded for losing only 3 of the 70 patients he treated during a spotted fever outbreak, most of whom he neglected to bill. In fact, he neglected to bill so many of his patients that his house was mortgaged to James Langdon many times over several years and he ultimately took possession when Dr. Lamb died. The two houses remained in the Langdon family until the death of James's daughter Lizzie in 1924. The brick house next became the property of Alton and Bertha Baird, and the lane running between the two homes became Baird Street, which is no longer a through street.

The City's Best-Dressed Carpenters

Baird was a carpenter who established a thriving construction business that was involved in many large projects throughout the city up until the 1970s, including the development of the town's first brick apartment building in 1930, which is still in operation today and can be seen in the background behind the inn.

Baird's crew of skilled carpenters assembled at the headquarters on Baird Street each morning, most in dress shirts and ties, over which they pulled coveralls before getting to work. My own grandfather, Nelson Paxman, was one of them.

One of their more whimsical projects was the construction of an enormous wooden model of the State House in 1929. It served as a parade float during the dedication of the Crown Point Bridge over Lake Champlain, when Vermont Governor John Weeks and New York Governor Franklin Roosevelt met in the middle to shake hands. The model State House went missing for a number of years in the 1980s, which is a story in itself that I won't get into, but thanks to the tireless detective work of one Paul H. Guare, it was located, restored and once more proudly rides through the streets of Montpelier in every parade. At all other times you can visit it at the Morse Farm and Sugar House, which is a few miles up Main Street in East Montpelier.

STOP 4.9 - MONTPELIER'S "ARMS DEALER"

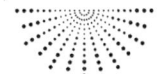

146 MAIN STREET

Across the street from the inn you'll see a brick house in the Greek Revival style. It was once the home of the famed Colonel Perley Pitkin. Along with being the fire chief and key partner in the Lane Manufacturing Company, he also served as the Quartermaster General for the state and had charge of the State Arsenal, which was filled with $600,000 worth of armaments supplied by the federal government. How did Montpelier come to have all that firepower?

It was given as compensation to the city in exchange for our agreement to allow the building of 25 hospital buildings in town to house Civil War soldiers suffering from injuries or disease. Both the Sloan Army Hospital and the arsenal were located on what is now College Street, up near the Vermont College of Fine Arts.

A few of the original hospital buildings still exist in the neighborhood, and one small building is left of the Arsenal and still goes by that name, although it is now privately owned. Because the impressive inventory of gunpowder, grenades and general military weaponry was rather more than the little town of Montpelier required, Colonel Pitkin was tasked with making a few sales to foreign governments, which an early history reports "materially aided the State treasury."

This plot of land, along with those of the next several buildings down, made up the property that was once owned by the Watrous family back in the very early 1800s. One of its family members – Sarah Watrous – is credited with a woodcut drawing of the town which is credited as the first rendered image of Montpelier. It was at the beginning of this book, but here it is again:

We are nearing the intersection of Main and School Streets now, and as you walk further in that direction you'll get a look at a few more examples of the variety and beauty of the city's architectural styles.

Montpelier's Own Doogie Hawser

Next to the Pitkin home is a lovely house built in what's known as the Gothic Revival Classic Cottage style, and after that is another Greek Revival beauty. That was built sometime before 1850 by James Spaulding, who was Montpelier's chief surgeon. This was a profession he decided to enter at the age of 7, and he came along so quickly that he was known as the "boy physician" in his native town of Sharon, Vermont. Finally, just before reaching the corner, you'll see two more gorgeous examples of the French Second Empire style. The one right next to the Unitarian Church belonged to James G. French, a wealthy merchant who built our first post office and also the largest city block on Main Street, which we'll see in Tour #5.

Welcome Back to Tour 3

It may seem like I'm skipping over the Trinity Methodist Church and the public library, but those two are covered in Tour #3. As you reach the intersection of School Street, we will also reach the end of this extended tour. You can peek around the corner and across the bridge to Elm Street where we started and see that our big looping walk is complete. If you stopped Tour #3 to follow the extended loop, you can pick it up where you left off, which is at Stop #3.5, where I tell you about the Unitarian Church we are in front of now.

When you are finished with Elm Street loops big and small, I hope to see you again for Tour #5!

TOUR 5 - STONECUTTERS WAY

A PATH BETWEEN BARS

Map for Stops 5.9 and 5.10 on page

STOP 5.1 - A DIVE FOR NICE PEOPLE

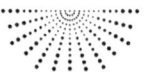

70 MAIN STREET, CHARLIE-O'S WORLD FAMOUS

*I*ntroduction
Welcome to the final installment of our walking tours around Montpelier. We have one more neighborhood to explore in this series. If you are thinking in terms of a roundtrip, this tour is a bit short of two miles, one up and one back, but it is all completely flat and easy walking, at least until we reach the end of Stonecutters Way. At that point, you may need to walk along the side of Barre Street for about a hundred yards to reach the last stop, but if it's any consolation, the last stop includes a bar! Let's get going!

So casual and secure is Charlie-O's in its own sense of worth that the category selected for its Facebook page is "Dive Bar." You have to admire that kind of self-confidence.

There are a couple of things I should clarify about the exterior signage. While it's true there's been a bar in this building since at least the early 1900s, Charlie-O's first opened its doors in 1976. Dating itself back to the War Between the States is just a bit of fun. As to the alluring "fine dining" promise stenciled on its awning? That's a cheerful, bald-faced lie. You might score a bag of chips inside, but unless you're desperate or completely insensible, I can't recommend the microwaveable items in the hanging basket above the bar. For some humor, you can see those items described on the menu next to the front door. The third promise of "good drinks and bad company"? That's absolutely true. No, I'm kidding. Yes, the drinks are great, but so is the company, and they feature live bands of every genre, from bluegrass to heavy metal.

In its earlier days, the place had a hard core biker bar reputation, and it was a brave punk rocker who ventured over the threshold. The choppers lined the block outside, and bodies did come flying out the door occasionally. These days, the vibe is more mellow. It's the church of all faiths - an eclectic mix of ages and backgrounds you would be hard-pressed to find anywhere else in town. So, check it out. You'll be fine. I'll wait for you in front of the fire station.

STOP 5.2 - THE FIREHOUSE THAT CAME AFTER THE FIRE

61 MAIN STREET

Flanking City Hall on one side is our fire station, and on the other is the Walgreens building, which is on the site where previously there was a brick building called the Lawrence Block. Its style was similar to the blocks you see on the opposite side of the street, but with an added fourth story.

On a winter night in 1924, a raging fire reduced the Lawrence Block to a smoking shell in a matter of hours. The eleven lives lost that night make it the single most devastating event in Montpelier's history to this day. The fact that several of the victims leapt to their death trying to escape the flames left the city traumatized and searching for answers.

At the time of the Lawrence Block fire, there was no centralized fire station. Responding to an alarm, call firemen had to spend precious minutes gathering pumpers and other gear from various storage sheds in the city before they could respond to whatever was in flames.

Within a year after this fire, however, the new firehouse was built, a new motorized hook and ladder truck had been purchased, and the city began a rapid transition to a fully staffed, full-time fire department. You may notice that the lane between City Hall and the fire station is called Pitkin Court. I promise this will be my final salute to the late great fire chief, Colonel Perley Pitkin, whose name I just love to keep reciting.

STOP 5.3 - MONTPELIER'S OWN BIG DIG

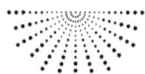

39 MAIN STREET CITY HALL PLAZA

*I*t's interesting to note that it wasn't until the beginning of the 20th century that Montpelier got around to thinking about a proper city hall building.

In 1909, citizens were finally persuaded by the Building Committee's argument, which exhorted "...the Capital of a state should not continue in the second century of its existence to lack what inferior cities possess, a building of its own..."

At the time there was a big open area here known as Haymarket Square, and once it was gone the city's farmers market disappeared with it until 1977, when it popped up again in the Court House parking lot. The construction on this site began in 1909 and it took the better part of two years to finish the building. One of the many sources of delay was an ill-timed sense of local pride. With the building only half-finished, the builders rushed to slap down a wooden floor so the city could host the Governor's Ball and avoid the humiliation of having it moved to a different town. The ball was a terrific success, but the floor buckled shortly after and had to be replaced with more expensive terrazzo.

It was all worth it, though. Today, our City Hall is second only to the State House in being an iconic symbol of Montpelier. Its yellow brick, Italian Renaissance style gives it the appearance of some grand Florentine palazzo, but inside there are a number of Ionic columns in the lobby to give it that little touch of Greek we loved so well. Lining the walls inside are some great old photographs of the city, and there is a public restroom inside as well.

World-Class Theater in the Capital City

It also has a large auditorium that is the home of the nonprofit Lost Nation Theater. Lost Nation has often been cited as one of the best regional theaters in the country. It offers a variety of musicals, drama and comedy in an annual season that runs from April to October. Tickets are available online at lostnationtheater.org

If you aren't there already, cross the street over to the City Hall side of Main Street at the Walgreens crosswalk, and turn to have a quick look at the impressive brick blocks lining the opposite side of the street. What's most amazing is that nearly all of them were built right after the second of Montpelier's two massive fires in 1875, with construction beginning as soon as the smoke had cleared. The largest is the French Block, identified by the central granite pediment on top.

James G. French, a wealthy local merchant who ran a clothing store and also served as the postmaster, had his building up and ready to occupy only 4 months after the fire. After its upper floors sat empty for several decades, a renovation has just been completed to create a new set of apartments in the French Block.

Eat, Drink and Shop

Our next destination is Barre Street, but before we leave this part of Main Street let's review a few of the restaurant choices available. You're maybe starting to realize you could be in Montpelier a couple of weeks and never eat in the same place twice. Next to Charlie-O's (which, again, not a dining option), we have the **Mad Taco** with its authentic and insanely tasty Mexican cuisine, along with a variety of hot sauce choices that can blow your head off. Next, right across from City Hall is **Pho Thai Express**, which has a large and yummy pan-Asian menu. Closer to the corner of Barre Street is **Bagitos**, another great choice for burritos, and also it's one of the few choices in town for bagels. It's right next to Montpelier's art-house cinema, the **Savoy**, where, along with seeing the movie, you can have some of the best organic popcorn you've ever tasted, and wash it down with a bottle of craft beer or glass of wine. On this side of the street, we've got the **China Star** for eating in or taking out all your familiar Chinese options. Further down and across the street from Shaw's is **Sarducci's**. This is Montpelier's wildly popular Italian restaurant, offering a riverside view and the most delicious polenta appetizer you've ever tasted. It sits at the beginning of Stonecutters Way, which we'll access from Barre Street a little farther up.

For shops on this stretch of Main Street you have **Bailey Road**, a bright, friendly boutique that advertises a shopping experience that's "like going through the closet of your most stylish friend." If you're looking for a quick fitness fix, you can book a spinning session at **Alpenglow** next door.

There's one other exciting development on this block that was still a work-in-progress as these tours went to press. **Rabble-Rouser** is a new worker-owned cooperative opening in the large space next to Alpenglow that promises to bring some added vibrance and activity to this end of the downtown area. Café, educational center, performance space, community gathering place, and chocolate!! All of it is still tantalizing hidden behind papered-over windows as I speak, but I know I will have more to say about it in the next edition!

Moving on now, the parking area in front of Capital Dry Cleaners is a good spot to stand for the next stop, where you can see a number of things at once while I describe them.

STOP 5.4 - BALDWIN'S LAST LAUGH & SOME RAILROAD TALK

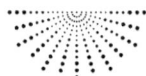

CORNER OF MAIN & BARRE STREETS

The first thing I'll talk about at this intersection is the bridge that extends over the Winooski. Traveling across and straight up the hill will eventually take you to Northfield, turning left will bring you to Barre, and turning right will put you back on I-89 to go wherever you want.

Until 1826, at this Main Street river crossing there were a series of bridges supported by trestles with wooden beams driven down into the riverbed. They were constantly being washed away. People would resort to small boats to get across but would more often be carried downstream by the river's swift current.

Then, a local inventor named Sylvanus Baldwin had an audacious idea for a bridge that wouldn't need any supporting trestles in the water beneath it.

He was heartily laughed at for his design, but it resulted in a long, covered bridge called the Old Red Arch that lasted for seventy years. It was replaced first by a steel truss bridge, similar in style to the railroad bridge you can see to the right behind Shaw's, and that gave way to the modern bridge you see now, which, ironically, is supported by concrete beams driven down into the riverbed.

Montpelier's "Other" Train Depot

It's not as lovely as the elegant station we once had on State Street, but the 3-story brick building on the left is the Main Street Train Depot, built around 1880. At one time it had train tracks running on both sides of it. The tracks you see today are the small branch line that led over that railroad bridge by Shaw's to the Montpelier Junction, which is near today's interstate. There, it connected to the main line of the Vermont Central Railroad that went to Burlington. The tracks on the other side that are gone now belonged to the Montpelier & Wells River Railroad. They ran along what is now Stonecutter's Way to Barre, and then on to Wells River where passengers could reconnect with the Vermont Central line or switch to the Boston & Maine.

The reason I'm telling you all this about railroads is because the Montpelier & Wells River line created a fast connection to Barre and its granite industry. When we return to Stonecutter's Way in a few minutes I'll explain the major impact that had on the development of this part of town and the city's overall economy.

Off the Beaten Path: If you are driving around with time on your hands, or if Northfield is on your itinerary (and it should be!), go straight across the bridge and up Northfield Street, and if you drive very slowly around the first curve you'll get a view of a fairytale cottage called "Athenwood". It was built in 1850 by Montpelier's most celebrated local artist, Thomas Waterman Wood. It was named after the Greek version of his wife's first name, and his own last name. We will learn a bit more about the artist and his interesting career in a few minutes.

Eat, Drink and Shop

Now let's walk up Barre Street, which you may have guessed takes you in the direction of the city it's named for. We are heading for the large church on the left. As we go, we'll pass yet another spot for grabbing a bite to eat. In the little red house on the right side of the street is **Buddy's Famous**, which offers quick service for either eating in or taking out hand-pressed burgers, hand-cut fries, and decadent milkshakes in assorted flavors.

STOP 5.5 - THE CROSS THAT DIDN'T BELONG

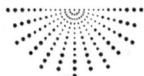

18 BARRE STREET, CHURCH OF SAINT AUGUSTINE

The cornerstone for this Gothic church was laid in 1892 when the parish began outgrowing its original brick church in an area near the State House.

It took 11 years to complete, is made of Barre granite, and if you think the towers to the left and right of the central door look a bit truncated, that's because they are. The square tower on the left was originally designed to rise a good 1 ½ stories above the central vault, and the one on the left was intended to be a slender steeple, but these were never completed.

THE YEAR THE KKK CAME TO CENTRAL VERMONT

The longest serving pastor was Monsignor William Crosby. He directed the parish for 41 years and is the only priest whose grave is on the church grounds, in a private area behind the shrine of Our Lady of Fatima. It was in the early years of his tenure that the Ku Klux Klan were briefly active in Montpelier, and in Vermont in general. The state had, and still has, a very small African-American population, so the group's harassment was more focused on citizens who were Catholic, Jewish or recent immigrants.

On one November evening in 1925, a group of Klansmen burned a ring of seven crosses on the hillsides surrounding Montpelier, including one in Hubbard Park and another in the Catholic Cemetery on upper Main Street. On that same night, Monsignor Crosby was roused in the middle of the night by a threatening, anonymous phone call which led him to discover that members of the Klan had also set fire to an oil-soaked cross on the steps of the church. It scarred the pavement with a scorched, oily stain that remained for years, but happily, the Klan's activities in Vermont did not.

It's a bit tricky predicting when the doors might be open, but the interior of the church is worth a visit, not so much for its design but for some of its features.

The original interior was traditionally Gothic, like its exterior. It had a wooden pulpit, altar rail, elaborately carved central and side altars, and beautifully stenciled walls.

The photos of it are breathtaking, but in 1968 it was completely remodeled in the Mid-Century Modern style, and in my opinion this was an unfortunate decision.

The Church's Works of Art

There are, however, some original elements remaining that hint at the glory that was. These include the large and very detailed sculptures of the Stations of the Cross, and the stained glass windows whose magnificence can only be appreciated from inside the church. They were created by the studio of Wilbur Burnham, a master artist who was also commissioned to produce 17 windows for the National Cathedral in Washington, DC. The Smithsonian identified Burnham's studio for stained glass as one of the four most accomplished in the country. The interior also features two original paintings by Thomas Waterman Wood hanging on the back wall on either side of the second-floor choir at the rear of the church. One is a copy of Raphael's Transfiguration, and the other a copy of Murillo's Madonna del Rosario. You could also pause to shed a tear over a remnant of the original wooden pulpit that's near the back of the left-side aisle as you face the altar.

The church is generally only open about an hour before Mass times, and for a short time afterwards. Mass times are Saturday at 4pm, Sunday at 7:45 and 10:00 am, and during the week there are sometimes Masses for special intentions at 8am and Noon.

At Times, Everyone Needs Alterations

We are going to continue walking up Barre Street, now. In its early years it was a tree-lined avenue filled with single family homes that had large gardens, hen coops and stables behind them, and after it was installed in 1898, the trolley line followed this route on its way to Barre. At #45, the Greek Revival painted white with red trim is the oldest on the street, and although it is sadly gone now, for most of my life the house had a sign next to the door that said "Alterations". This sounds metaphysical, but it was only advertising the services of the seamstress who lived there for more than half a century. Across from it is our next stop.

STOP 5.6 - THE SELF-TAUGHT MASTER

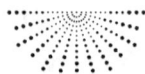

46 BARRE STREET, TW WOOD GALLERY

*T*his 3-story brick building was constructed after the 1927 flood as a convent for the Sisters of Mercy, who were the teachers for the St. Michael's Catholic School. The large brick building across the driveway was added in 1931 to serve as the high school, and the more modern building attached to the back of the convent was added in 1959 to house the elementary school students. Today, the high school is the home of a very lively Senior Activity Center, with a mix of subsidized and market rate apartments on the upper floors.

A MUST-SEE GALLERY IN MONTPELIER

The convent is now the Center for Arts and Learning, offering practice and work spaces for musicians and artists. Although the Catholic school closed several years ago, there is still an independent K-8 school operating here, and it is also the site of the TW Wood Art Gallery, which has changing exhibits featuring the works of both Montpelier artists and those from other parts of Vermont. If you are interested at all in art this should definitely be on you itinerary, and I'll tell you a bit about its namesake, now. He is one of Montpelier's most acclaimed historical figures, and a nationally recognized artist who once served as President of both the National Academy of Design and the American Watercolor Society.

Thomas Waterman Wood was born in Montpelier in 1823. He apparently became inspired by the work of a traveling portrait painter, which was a common occupation in the days before photography. At that time in Montpelier there weren't many people who knew much about art, and certainly no formal education available, so he was largely self-taught, using supplies and books that a friend from Boston occasionally provided.

As an adult, Wood studied in Boston for a short period and began his career as a portrait painter, but he returned to Vermont to marry his wife Minerva Robinson, and they moved into the fairytale cottage I mentioned earlier called Athenwood (the Latin name for Minerva is Athena).

After extensive travel in Europe, they settled permanently in New York City, but they maintained a presence in Montpelier, and Wood's art continuously drew on the places and people he'd known growing up here.

He made his living with portraits, but it's the storytelling "genre paintings" that are best loved. This is a style that's most famously associated with Norman Rockwell – scenes of everyday life in New England that depict vivid, realistically drawn characters.

Wood found himself behind enemy lines during the Civil War, and lived for several years in Tennessee and Kentucky. He is perhaps the first American painter who incorporated African Americans as central subjects in a way that avoided racial stereotyping.

While contemporary artists typically represented this population as slaves and servants hovering as stock background figures, Wood's paintings are pointedly different, depicting various demographics and subjects and conveying a sense of the dignity and personality of each.

The gallery has limited public viewing hours, which is a shame, but if you can fit in a visit any time between Noon and 4pm Tuesday through Saturday, you won't regret it.

Seniors in High School to Seniors in Life

As we move up the street to the next large brick building you can just make out the original lettering for Saint Michael's High School over the front door. At the top is the likeness of Michael the Archangel himself, carved in stone, and the small pediment over his head once held a cross fashioned from concrete. This was remodeled several years ago to serve as a Senior Activity Center, and it also has both subsidized senior housing and market rate apartments on the upper floors.

Cross at the crosswalk, and you'll arrive in front of the Recreational Center, which was constructed in 1932 as a state armory for Vermont's Army National Guard. Next to it is the path we are going to take to reach Stonecutters Way, but we'll continue just a bit farther up the street for two final stops before leaving Barre Street.

The first is the red-shingled house in the Gothic Cottage style that is the second one past the Recreational Center.

STOP 5.7 - MONTPELIER'S DEEP-ROOTED IMMIGRANT COMMUNITY

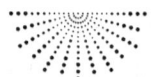

63 BARRE STREET

In many of these tours, when talking about the people who shaped the development of Montpelier I've cited many names with a solid Yankee pedigree and ancestors who came from the colonial states of southern New England. It's now important to mention the city's vibrant early immigrant life, which was largely centered in the neighborhood we are in now. Italians, French Canadians and the Irish all gravitated to Barre Street. It was a collection of close-knit tribes loosely stitched into a community, and in many of the backyards along this street you can still find some of the wild grapevines that were cultivated to make rough red wines and grappa. Many of the residents were highly skilled stonecutters who came from the northern regions of Italy to work in the granite sheds of Barre and Montpelier. Their lives were poignantly captured by Mari Tomasi, the novelist who was born in this house in 1907 and lived in it until her death.

A Storyteller for Stonecutters

Her parents came to Montpelier from Turin, Italy, and throughout her life Mari embraced her cultural heritage. She remained single all her life, working as a newspaper editor and writing for magazines while she helped to care for her large, extended family. In good weather, when she could snatch a few hours of free time, she could be found in the back garden of this house with a typewriter propped on the stump of a tree, working on her first novel. *Deep Grow the Roots* was published in 1940. It was set in Italy during the time of Mussolini's rise to power, and although received well, her second novel, released nine years later, is considered her best work. *Like Lesser Gods* is set in the fictional

"Granitetown", which is modeled on the city of Barre. It's an immigrant story centered around the lives of a particular family, but on a deeper level it's a story full of symbolism for the deep, almost mystical bond the stonecutters feel for the granite they shape, and the tragic irony that dedication to their craft doomed many of them to a slow, suffocating death.

Dying Too Young

Mari would have been familiar with the granite industry through interactions with neighbors and customers at her parents' grocery store on Main Street, but she gained deeper insights during the years of the Depression, while conducting oral history interviews with Barre's granite workers for the Works Progress Administration. Alongside the stories of community life and beautiful stonework there is an underlying thread of tragedy and hardship, primarily caused by the tuberculo-silicosis that afflicted so many of those who worked in the poorly ventilated sheds. The swirling granite dust inhaled during the polishing process were like tiny shards of glass that slowly tore their lungs apart. Modern technology eventually resulted in methods of removing the dust from the work areas, but not in time for the earlier generations who died too young. Mari Tomasi also left us prematurely. She died of cancer at the age of 58 in 1965. Her papers are on file with the University of Vermont, and some of the oral history interviews were published posthumously in 2003 under the title *Men Against Granite*.

Although most of the area's granite industry is centered near the Barre quarries, there were sheds in Montpelier as well, where memorials were carved and polished. They were concentrated at the eastern end of Barre Street on a stretch of land between the railroad and the Winooski River. One of them remains there still, and we'll see it a bit later.

ONE FINAL BAKERY VISIT!

Before we begin our walk along Stonecutters Way, there's one more stop in this area you should not miss if you are here any time between 7:30am and 2:00pm Wednesday through Sunday. I have made it my mission to provide you with a bakery stop on almost every tour in this series, and this is the last, but by no means least. **Bohemian Bakery** is less than a hundred feet up the street from this spot, at the corner of Hubbard and Barre Street.

Like Birchgrove Baking, which is highlighted in Tour 4, this bakery is also on the site of a former neighborhood store called Steve's Market. For over 25 years, the white-aproned Steve Cano held court from his butcher block, and neighbors could have their balance penciled onto a notepad at the register for monthly invoicing. The folks at Bohemian put out a big colorful "Open" flag when they are ready for customers. If you see it flying, you'd be a fool to not hustle up there and get a taste of something.

I won't come along because I actually live in this neighborhood, so I visit that bakery more than is good for me. When you're done there, make your way back to the lane next to the Rec Center. Walk all the way down, across the railroad tracks, and over to the bike path on Stonecutters Way. I will be waiting there for you, away from the scene of temptation.

STOP 5.8 - REMEMBERING OUR CITY IN THE RAILROAD TIMES

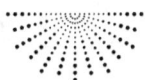

STONECUTTERS WAY, BEHIND THE RECREATIONAL CENTER

We've arrived at Stonecutters Way, and as you face the river, you can see the back of Sarducci's restaurant on your right, and on the left a long straight path stretching into the distance that ends at Granite Street. That is the direction we are taking, and you can start walking while I talk because we won't have another reason to stop for a while. This sidewalk that we are on serves as part of the city's bike path. It begins a few miles northwest of here, not far from the Montpelier Junction train station, and it runs more or less parallel to the train tracks all the way through town. Even as I speak, there's a project underway to expand the path farther south in the direction of Barre. I'm not sure when they'll be finished, so near the end of this tour the walking route might get a bit more creative.

Montpelier's Boom Times

You maybe noticed there was only one set of tracks to cross before reaching the sidewalk, but right up until the early 1990s, this entire area from Main to Granite Street comprised the Winooski East Railyard and it was chock-a-block with crisscrossing rail lines and various sheds and machine shops.

Along with the passenger service lines, there were several railroad companies operating freight cars that rumbled through these yards several times a day. In the early 1900s there were no attractive hedges and fences separating the works from the houses along Barre Street, so it was truly a very busy industrial part of the city. This area, along with the Lane Manufacturing complex on the other side of town, were the biggest symbols of the city's economic growth during this time.

Across the river, the opposite riverbank is where the town of Berlin began, and although the stretch of Berlin Street that you see at this end was a tree-lined avenue at the end of the

19th century, the area past the intersection with Main Street was lined with buildings and mills making cotton, carriages, and a gruesome sounding elixir called Greene's Syrup of Tar. It was guaranteed to quiet

your cough, which isn't hard to believe since it was spiked with heroin.

Things had calmed down quite a bit when I was growing up on this street in the late 60s and early 70s, but I still remember my father coming home from work through the back yard, after catching a ride on the steps of a freight engine, and I never got tired of walks along the tracks to peer into sidelined box cars and an old red caboose that had grass growing up around it.

I can wax nostalgic, but what we have here today is really much better. The modern buildings you pass along the riverbank are on the sites of old railyard structures, extensively redeveloped into office space.

Turntable Park

As you walk, you'll see some granite pillars that have informational plaques about the history of the area. Unfortunately they haven't weathered well and are in need of renovation, but just before you reach the parking lot for the Hunger Mountain Co-op, you'll see one in pretty good shape next to Turntable Park, a small green space tucked between two of the redeveloped buildings. It serves as a reminder of the industrial roots of this area. When in operation, the railroad turntable was used to rotate a locomotive and send it off again, either in a different direction or into the engine house that sat just to the left of it.

The engine house was the last structure to be redeveloped along this stretch of riverbank. Once retired from railroad use, it was known for a while as the Salt Shed for the road salt that was stored here. It was also briefly used as an indoor skating rink and considered as a site for an arts center before being sold for private development. It now houses the Nature Conservancy and the offices of the Vermont State Colleges System.

TOUR 5 MAP (CONTINUED)

STOP 5.9 - GOT ANY HEADY?

623 STONECUTTERS WAY, HUNGER MOUNTAIN CO-OP

*H*ere near the end of Stonecutters Way, we've arrived at Montpelier's cooperatively owned grocery store, Hunger Mountain Co-op, which has been in the city in a few different locations since the late 1960s. For much of its existence, it was not really considered a must-see attraction in Montpelier, but that was before the golden age of Vermont beer got rolling.

Starting around 2011, The Alchemist Restaurant in Waterbury single-handedly revived the aluminum beer can when it began distributing a staggeringly popular IPA called Heady Topper. They did almost no advertising, but it quickly became an award-winner and a national sensation. The Alchemist had a pretty limited production capacity in its early days, so the beer was only available in small quantities on certain days, in certain stores. Our

Co-op was one such store and its sleepy anonymity disappeared almost overnight.

Craft beer fans from all over the country started showing up at the crack of dawn to form a line that snaked all the way down the parking lot, just for a chance to fill the trunk of their car with a few cases of "Heady". Once they were here, they discovered Vermont was an absolute paradise of hand-crafted beer, and more breweries were popping up all the time, so the Co-op quickly became a required stop on the beer trail. These days Heady is slightly easier to come by, but the store has a pretty impressive selection of other brews as well, both local and beyond.

If beer isn't your thing, they also have an amazing array of cheeses and a fantastic hot and cold buffet with a cafe-style seating area. I definitely recommend checking it out before we get back on the path to our next stop at the intersection with Granite Street.

STOP 5.10 - SOMEBODY HAD TO MAKE THEM

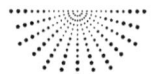

717 STONECUTTERS WAY

This blue-painted building with white trim is deceiving to look at from this angle because you are only seeing the side of it. When you continue across Granite Street you get a better notion of the full size of it. It's considered one of Vermont's best-preserved wood-framed factory buildings from the early 20th century, and on this site it manufactured the same small household item by the million, beginning in 1918. That small household item? The clothespin.

Cross-Town Competition

It turns out in the mid-to-late 19th century, Vermonters virtually had a monopoly on the patents for clothespin design, and you may be surprised to hear that Montpelier was the home to not just one, but two factories that churned out these handy little devices. The one at this site was the National Clothespin Factory, and downstream, on the opposite side of the river near Main Street was the US Clothespin Company. To power their machinery, they created the original dam on the site of the one you see today from the Main Street Bridge.

The two companies enjoyed a healthy rivalry for several years with their slightly different designs, but the National survived long after the other had closed. The business was purchased by local businessman Wayland Jack Crowell in 1965, and he was able to push the production to 38 million clothespins a year.

At some point during his tenure, he walked across Granite Street to the Northeast Granite Company, which is still in operation today, and designed his own gravestone. You can see it at the Middlesex Center cemetery - a five-foot long granite clothespin. When the company finally closed in 2003, it was the last remaining producer of wooden clothespins in the country.

WHERE THE WALKING ROUTE BECOMES SPORTY

Now, as we cross Granite Street, you'll see a bike path running parallel to Barre Street that might not yet be paved. There may also be a spot where you have to walk on the side of the road for about a hundred yards to reach our next stop, which is Gin Lane. If it's getting on toward twilight when you reach this point I wouldn't recommend it because night-time in this neighborhood is VERY dark, but if its during the day it's fine.

STOP 5.11 - YOU WON'T BELIEVE WHATS ON TAP!

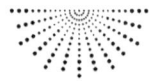

GIN LANE

The large open field you see on the opposite side of Barre Street here is called Sabin's Pasture, named after the 19th century

Montpelier businessman Charles Sabin, who operated a slate quarry here for several years which focused exclusively on supplying contractors with slate roofing. Today, it's one of the city's last undeveloped land parcels of significant size, so as you can imagine, it is frequently a topic of lively, sometimes heated discussion.

GIN LANE - WE'VE ARRIVED!

On this side of the street is the city's newest addition - the Caledonia Spirits Distillery, which produces Barr Hill Gin. If you don't already know about their secret ingredient I'm not going to give away the surprise you are in for. There are free tours at 1:00 and 3:00 each day.

There's no restaurant but they have food trucks right by the front door from Tuesday through Sunday selling pizza, barbecue and seafood on alternating days. They also have a gorgeous long bar and an outdoor patio, and as if that wasn't enough, they have gin & tonics and Moscow mules ON TAP! Is it any wonder that I planned this as the last stop on the last of our tours around Montpelier? It's a good thing we're walking right?!

Cheers!

DON'T GO YET

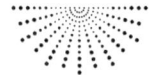

*O*h, wait, wait!
I have a few people to thank before we start down Gin Lane. First is you, of course. Thank you for being so interested in my hometown that you wanted to learn more about it. I hope you've enjoyed the tours as much as I enjoyed making them.

I'd also like to thank Paul Carnahan and Bill Fish, who wrote *Montpelier: Images of Vermont's Capital City*, and also Paul Heller, who wrote *Montpelier Chronicles: Historic Stories of the Capital City*. Both of these books helped me enormously. They are fantastic sources of local history, full of old photos and interesting stories. To get the full details on the highlights I've provided here, you can buy them at Bear Pond Books on Main Street, and you should!

My thanks also to the Montpelier Heritage Group, both for the good works it did in advocating for the restoration of many of our historic buildings, and also for their increasingly rare booklets, *A Walk Through Montpelier* and *A Second Walk Through Montpelier*. You may be able to find them at the Kellogg-Hubbard Library.

I'm also grateful to my fellow Board members in the Montpelier Historical Society. They approved the disbursement of funds that made this project possible.

I'm especially grateful to my mother and first reader, Claire Guare, who provided corrections and a gentle nudge when she thought things needed to move along faster.

And finally, a thank you and a dedication: to my father Paul H. Guare, a.k.a., Mr. Montpelier. I wish I'd paid more attention all those times you put on your local historian hat, but now at long last I see the point of it all, and I hope you'd think I've done right by the place.

And now, for real this time - Cheers!

THE MODEL STATE HOUSE ON ITS MAIDEN VOYAGE

Paul H Guare and his brother Richard, 1929

www.ingramcontent.com/pod-product-compliance
Lightning Source LLC
Chambersburg PA
CBHW070738020526
44118CB00035B/1483